THE ONLY
SHADOW
WORK
WORKBOOK
YOU NEED

33+ Exercises & Journal Prompts To Help You Integrate Your Shadow For Inner Child Healing, Trauma Recovery & Authentic Self-Discovery

10 EXTRA MATERIALS INCLUDED INSIDE

LAUREN. J. ABRAHAM

CONTENTS

PAGES

INTRODUCTION

> "The wound is the place where the light enters you.
>
> — Rumi"

We find ourselves amidst contrasting forces, almost like two sides of a coin. Yet, upon closer examination, it becomes evident that these forces often complement each other. As we explore the complexities of our identities, it becomes apparent that there is more than meets the eye. Indeed, as individuals, we possess facets that go beyond the surface. Many of us harbor a hidden side, often referred to as our "shadow self," which, despite being a significant aspect of our being, we tend to conceal.

I am driven by a resolute passion to aid beginners in navigating the subtle intricacies of their subconscious. My commitment stems from both personal experiences and an earnest desire to empower others on their path to healing. Through this book, I extend to you a methodical guide, drawn from my own journey of self-discovery and shaped by a keen understanding of the nuances of shadow work.

In the recesses of our minds, shadows linger, casting subtle influences on our thoughts and actions. Have you contemplated the obscured facets of your personality, those silent architects shaping your life's narrative? The journey we take within these pages is an exploration of these concealed realms—a disciplined odyssey into the realm of self-awareness through the lens of shadow work.

Allow me to share a personal vignette that serves as the genesis of my commitment to shadow work. It was a moment of profound realization, a recognition that the uncharted corners of my psyche held the key to unlocking a life of authenticity and emotional mastery. This pivotal moment, coupled with witnessing the transformative power of shadow work in my own life and the lives of others, kindled the flame of dedication that propels this book.

But why should you delve into the complexities of shadow work?

This book is crafted with a singular purpose—to furnish beginners with a methodical and accessible guide for navigating the intricacies of their inner selves. It serves as a roadmap, leading you through the nuances of understanding and practicing shadow work, using a variety of strategies and journal prompts to demystify the process.

The concept of shadow work and the shadow self often elicits negative associations. Some might envision Peter Pan's mischievous shadow, a primitive counterpart to the storybook hero, making situations worse. Others may think of a haunting shadow lurking around corners or a dark side that taps into our more sinister nature.

However, understanding shadow work and the shadow self reveals a less intimidating reality. In fact, these concepts offer profound insights into how we understand and manage our emotions, as well as our perceptions of ourselves and the world.

Coined by the Swiss founder of analytical psychology, Carl Jung, the idea behind shadow work is that each of us harbors repressed or neglected aspects of ourselves. These forgotten facets of our personalities, the parts we've chosen to reject, constitute our shadow self.

According to retired psychotherapist Natacha Duke, "The parts we hide from ourselves are not inherently good or bad … they're just a part of who we are" (Cleveland Clinic, 2023). Despite our rejection, these aspects linger in our unconscious, integral to our core sense of self. It becomes our responsibility to explore and unearth these suppressed elements. Through shadow work, we can learn to embrace these concealed aspects, integrating them into our overall identity in the pursuit of becoming whole.

Describing shadow work as addressing blind spots, Duke emphasizes on how the shadow self often originates in childhood, shaped by messages that certain aspects of ourselves are undesirable or unlovable. For instance, if you were a talkative child repeatedly told to be quiet, you might suppress that talkative side to feel accepted. Over time, these repressed traits manifest in triggered emotional reactions or unexpected outbursts.

Duke underscores the importance of addressing these blind spots, stating, "What we resist persists." Unresolved issues from the shadow self can surface in relationships, leading to conflicts triggered by traits we have suppressed.

Consider the example of valuing generosity but harboring repressed feelings of selfishness in the shadow self. Encounter someone prioritizing themselves, and you might be triggered, creating conflicts despite the other person's actions being neither right nor wrong.

At its essence, shadow work involves understanding your triggers, uncovering their root causes, and fostering self-acceptance. Duke emphasizes the beauty in all parts of oneself, stressing that the shadow self doesn't inherently hold negativity but can unlock new and exciting dimensions of one's personality actively avoided until now (Cleveland Clinic, 2023).

To traverse the depths of shadow work, this guide is divided into five distinct parts. Commencing with foundational principles in the initial section, we progress systematically through different facets of subconscious exploration, culminating in the synthesis of your discoveries. Each part builds upon the last, offering a seamless progression toward emotional mastery.

This book is tailored for beginners—those who may approach the concept of shadow work with a mix of curiosity and trepidation. If you find yourself standing at the threshold of your inner self, uncertain of the shadows that may be revealed, rest assured that this guide is designed with your needs in mind. It serves as a gentle companion, providing support as you navigate the uncharted waters of self-discovery.

From increased self-awareness, healing from past traumas, and heightened emotional intelligence, this book serves as the key to unlocking transformative outcomes, offering the tools and insights necessary for meaningful self-discovery.

With an open heart and a willingness to explore the depths within, turn the page and commence this journey. Embrace the challenges, uncertainties, and revelations that await. Your initial step into the world of shadow work is a profound one, a step toward a more authentic and fulfilling life.

Remember that the shadows not only harbor echoes of your fears but also bear the seeds of your strength. With each revelation, you unveil a truer version of yourself. I hold a firm belief in the transformative power of shadow work, and I am eager for you to witness the profound changes it can bring into your life. Let this book be your guide in the darkness, leading you toward the light of emotional mastery.

CHAPTER 1:
SHEDDING LIGHT ON SHADOW WORK

> *But that shadow has been serving you! What hurts you, blesses you.*
> *Darkness is your candle. Your boundaries are your quest.*
> *You must have shadow and light source both.*
> *Listen, and lay your head under the tree of awe.*
> *– Rumi*

When everyone around us seems to be facing the same challenge, perhaps it's time for some introspection? It's like a shadow that keeps reappearing in our lives, causing frustration. Embracing this simple truth is like unlocking the door to freedom—the freedom to bring about meaningful change in our lives.

Let's imagine it as preparing for a major celebration, like the anticipation before Diwali. Before welcoming the light and joy, there's a tradition of clearing out our homes. Why? Because, to truly revel in life and celebrate who we are, we need to sweep away the clutter—the remnants of our past, unproductive habits, and shadows within.

Just as we sometimes overlook the mess within our homes, we may also neglect our internal struggles. It's akin to acknowledging a glitch in the system once we've exhausted blaming our past and others. Taking responsibility for our internal chaos becomes the key to unlocking the door to self-improvement.

If it feels like everyone around us is facing challenges, it might be worth considering if the root of the issue lies within ourselves. What we fail to recognize within ourselves could be mirrored in the challenges we see around us.

So, are you ready for this journey of self-discovery, my friend? It's about acknowledging our imperfections, finding common ground, and understanding our shared humanity. Only then can we truly connect with others and celebrate the beautiful mess that is life.

WHAT IS A SHADOW?

Think of the shadow as that part of ourselves that hasn't seen the light of our awareness—it's like our personal uncharted territory. It encompasses our lingering wounds, unresolved relationships, and even the persistent struggles that we can't quite shake off, but it's also our hidden powerhouse—our Inner Gold.

It could be that irritating or triggering trait in us, or even something we admire in others. This whole concept comes from the brilliant mind of Swiss psychiatrist Carl Jung. The shadow is basically the mysterious, unexplored, or not-so-accepted side of our personality—

the dark stuff we tend to push down, deny, or keep hidden. And guess what? What we try to push away ends up sticking around in our unconscious, whether it's our own personal one or the collective one we share.

Our shadow isn't all rational and thought-out; it's instinctive and shows up in our dreams, projections, and those little irritations we can't ignore. It's like this silent puppeteer that influences our choices and behavior. Sometimes, we might wear masks or build walls around ourselves, thinking we're keeping it at bay or trying to compensate for it. But the truth is, the shadow won't really disappear until we face it head-on, deal with it, and heal from it.

Ever heard the saying, "We don't see things as they are, we see them as we are"? It's attributed to Anaïs Nin, but the sentiment aligns with the Babylonian Talmud too. Engaging with our shadows is an ongoing journey, and it's a bit like every person and thing having a shadow. The brighter the light, the more noticeable the shadow. Even every archetype has its own shadowy side—the stronger the light, the darker the shadow.

Your inner shadow encompasses the aspects of yourself that you subconsciously reject. This concept was popularized by the Carl Jung, who introduced the idea of the shadow self within the framework of the collective unconscious, consisting of various Jungian archetypes:

1. Self: The center of the personality or psyche, representing conscious awareness.
2. Shadow: The dark and emotional facet of the psyche.
3. Anima: An idealized image of a woman that connects individuals to their feminine side.
4. Animus: A part of the psyche capable of reflection and self-awareness.
5. Persona: The mask worn to present oneself to the world while safeguarding the inner self.
6. Hero: A psychological component able to conquer evil and destruction.
7. Wise Old Man: A personification of the self that holds wisdom.
8. Trickster: A childlike aspect of the psyche seeking gratification.

Jung described the shadow archetype as the darker, emotional side of one's personality, noting that it could be perceived as inferior or immoral, although not necessarily so.

Consider a scenario where, as a child, you were teased for being talkative. Developing a belief that you "talk too much," you may withdraw within, carefully assessing every conversation to avoid being perceived as overly chatty. When someone innocently comments about the number of words on a presentation slide, it triggers an intense emotional response. The anger stems not from the comment itself but from the part of you emotionally invested in avoiding the label of a chatterbox. Anything that brings your shadow self into the light is seen as a threat to your identity and, ultimately, your sense of safety.

What makes up your shadow is shaped by what you unconsciously reject within yourself, often manifesting as negative self-talk. These rejected aspects are frequently rooted in childhood experiences.

Shadows in our lives are like imprints from our early days, especially when just one moment can etch a lasting mark on our subconscious mind. It's those times in childhood when we felt judged, shamed, small, or like we didn't quite measure up—basically, when we felt anything but good enough or worthy. And it's in those moments that our light dims, and our shadows start to take shape.

Sometimes, it's the result of not-so-great parenting—maybe it was abusive, controlling, or laced with passive aggression. Parents with traits such as being overly disciplinary, puritanical, or even narcissistic can cast a long shadow over our development. When you add in those childhood rules and messages, it's like faulty programming, creating these glitches that manifest in dysfunctional behavior—such as patterns of anger, abuse, or manipulation. It's almost like a software bug in the system of our personalities. Crazy how those early experiences can stick with us, right?

One arena where our shadows tend to surface prominently is in our close relationships, be it within our family or as parents. It's like a breeding ground for triggers, pushing us to our limits and offering the maximum potential for personal growth.

Yet, the flip side is that if we don't address these shadows, they can wreak havoc in our relationships—leading to estrangement or conflicts. It's like an unavoidable part of our life script, almost like a karmic tie that binds us to these challenging dynamics.

Sure, we could navigate life by carefully tiptoeing around our triggers, but let's face it, growth seldom happens within the confines of our comfort zone. Life has this funny way of shaking things up through shadow conflicts, forcing us to confront our deepest insecurities and fears.

Can you think about that friend, or a dear one, who always seems to end up in similar relationship dramas? Or that colleague who jumps from one job to another, yet somehow, the same issues persist. It's like we carry these unlearned lessons with us, recreating the same dynamics, sometimes even across lifetimes.

Now, imagine this, when we're finally ready to confront our shadows, that's when the echoes of our darker moments surface. Yet, for many, it's more comfortable to linger in victimhood, avoiding the responsibility for the mess we find ourselves in and the one we unknowingly create for others. The shadow side has this uncanny ability to influence every choice we make, often taking control in areas where we least expect it. This can sadly manifest in addictions, self-sabotage, and self-harm.

Take, for instance, the common example of busyness or workaholism, especially prevalent in men, as a modern addiction and self-harm pattern. It all starts with disconnecting from our emotions and intuition (the Yin-Yang/Anima-Animus dynamic). The consequence? Relationship disasters, a pervasive toxic masculinity or femininity, and an unsettling dark side to ambition—greed and passion devoid of compassion. It's a pattern that we witness all around us, and it's a stark reminder of how our shadows can cast a long, sometimes damaging, influence on our lives.

Shadows reside within both our unconscious and subconscious realms, contributing to the difficulty in managing triggers through the conscious mind or sheer willpower, let alone achieving their healing. The initial step involves cultivating awareness of our triggers through mindfulness. However, the crucial aspect entails actively engaging with our intricate and concealed personality traits, often conflicting with one another. To navigate this process effectively, the assistance of a knowledgeable guide becomes indispensable, someone capable of steering us through this intricate terrain and ultimately facilitating the healing of our dark side.

WHAT IS SHADOW WORK?

Shadow work is like peeling back the layers of our hidden self, often called the "shadow self." It's that part of our unconscious mind where thoughts, emotions, or memories deemed as unacceptable linger in the shadows of our awareness. These "shadows" tend to be buried deep, carrying the weight of shame, negativity, or arising from challenging life experiences.

Imagine it as a journey of deepening self-awareness, an exploration into the side of ourselves that usually stays tucked away—the "shadow side." Sometimes, it's about embracing the darker corners within to illuminate the path toward the light.

Let me share something personal. I've struggled with my own shadows, those moments of self-doubt and insecurities that seemed too daunting to face. It's like carrying a hidden backpack of emotions that influenced my choices and relationships more than I realized. If you've ever felt that tug of unease or a weight you can't quite name, you might be familiar with the shadows too.

Carl Jung described personality using four archetypes, with one being the "shadow." This inner shadow is like a label for the part of ourselves we tend to keep tucked away or repressed. While it might feel unfavorable, Jung saw the shadow as an indispensable aspect of who we are. This inner shadow could be a reflection of inner insecurities, bottled-up anger, subconscious negativity, or even profound trauma. It's like the darker hues of our life experiences, sometimes challenging to face.

And now, in the realm of shadow work, we're delving into those thoughts, feelings, and experiences that we've pushed down or hidden away. Why? It's a journey toward a deeper understanding of ourselves, a means to enhance our connections with others, a process of learning more about the essence of who we are, and a pathway to healing from past traumas.

I recently met someone who, due to a childhood incident of being constantly criticized, developed an inner shadow of unworthiness. This shadow impacted their choices, relationships, and self-perception. Through shadow work, they could unearth and heal this hidden wound, fostering a profound transformation toward self-acceptance and empowerment.

If you've ever felt like there's something holding you back, something you can't quite put your finger on, you're not alone. Shadow work is a journey we can take together, a personal exploration that holds the potential for growth, self-discovery, and healing—the kind of journey that makes us more compassionate, not just with ourselves, but with others too.

SHADOW WORK AND JUNGIAN PSYCHOLOGY

Renowned psychoanalyst Carl Jung introduced a fascinating concept—the "shadow self." This term encapsulates those aspects individuals tend to repress or consciously avoid acknowledging. Jung proposed that this shadow self serves as a counterweight to the persona—the public face that individuals present to the world.

It's essential to note that, while the shadow self can harbor negative impulses like anger and resentment, Jung believed it harbored positive potentials, such as creativity. He considered the shadow self integral to one's experience of the world and the dynamics of their relationships.

Jung posited that individuals could achieve a deeper understanding of themselves and cultivate balance by actively engaging with their shadow self. This notion lays the foundation for what we now refer to as "shadow work," rooted in Jungian psychology.

According to Jung, a person's personality comprises the persona, the outward face presented to the public, and the shadow self, a more private and concealed aspect. Unlike the persona, the shadow often encompasses traits that an individual prefers to keep hidden. Crucially, Jung did not perceive the shadow as a negative or shameful component of one's personality; instead, he regarded it as a crucial part of the psyche.

The objective of shadow work is to integrate the shadow and the persona. This process empowers individuals to develop the skills to manage impulses typically overlooked, such as anger or greed.

Jung also asserted that the collective unconscious plays a significant role in influencing the shadow. This concept refers to the shared memories and impulses of society as a whole. Consequently, Jung's framework accommodates systemic issues such as racism within the notion of the shadow self.

In the same vein, just as engaging in shadow work aids in addressing aspects of one's personality usually avoided, Jung envisioned that it could enable individuals to confront prejudices and impulses stemming from broader social challenges. It's a profound journey of self-discovery and societal understanding, and if you're considering delving into it, know that you're not alone—I'm here to help guide you through this transformative process.

CHALLENGES ARISING FROM UNACKNOWLEDGED SHADOWS

Jung delved deeply into the shadow's nuances, recognizing its profound impact on interpersonal dynamics, group dynamics, and even on a global scale. Failure to recognize, acknowledge, and address shadow elements often underlies issues between individuals, within groups, and across societies. Understanding and integrating the shadow is a vital aspect of therapeutic relationships, individuation, and the journey toward a more enriched and authentic self.

Reflecting on your own experiences, can you identify instances where lack of awareness about your own shadow affected your interactions with others, and how did it impact those relationships?

THE SHADOW'S ROLE IN SHAPING IDENTITY

Complementary to Jung's concept of the persona, representing "what oneself as well as others thinks one is," the shadow embodies the concealed, often inferior, and guilt-laden aspects of personality. Contrary to the belief that the shadow is solely a source of morally reprehensible tendencies, it also harbors positive qualities like normal instincts, appropriate reactions, realistic insights, and creative impulses.

How do you perceive the interplay between your persona and your shadow in shaping your identity, and can you identify specific instances where your shadow qualities have influenced your self-perception?

UNLOCKING THE POTENTIAL WITHIN THE SHADOW

It is crucial to emphasize that the shadow encompasses diverse qualities, capacities, and potential. Failure to recognize and embrace these aspects maintains a state of impoverishment, depriving individuals of energy sources and meaningful connections with others. Therapy plays a pivotal role in challenging belief systems, reconnecting with suppressed aspects, and promoting personal growth.

Considering your own journey, can you identify aspects within your own shadow that, if acknowledged, could lead to personal growth and improved relationships?

PERSONAL AND COLLECTIVE DIMENSIONS OF THE SHADOW

Understanding the shadow involves considering both personal and collective aspects. The personal shadow, often perceived as black, formless, and unwanted, coexists with the collective shadow, shaped by cultural influences. Recognizing these shadows is essential for navigating the complexities of shared values and understanding cultural differences.

EXPLORING THE SHADOW'S DEPTHS: EVIL AND PROJECTION

Diving into the deepest layers of the shadow reveals manifestations of evil in the world. The shadow is often encountered through projection onto others, both external individuals/groups and internal dream figures. This process of projection can be a defense mechanism against disowned aspects of one's psychosomatic unity, such as issues related to the body, sexuality, and emotions.

Reflecting on your own experiences, can you recall instances where your judgments or dislikes of others were actually projections of aspects within yourself that you struggle with, and how did this realization influence your self-perception?

INFLUENCE OF OTHERS ON THE SHADOW: DEVELOPMENT AND REPRESSION

From infancy through adolescence, individuals absorb messages from caregivers about acceptability in terms of body, feelings, and behavior. Unacceptable traits become repressed, forming the shadow. The internalization of caregivers' attitudes toward these undesirable qualities intensifies the hostility toward the shadow, often leading to feelings of shame.

Can you identify specific messages from caregivers that influenced the formation of your shadow, and how have these influences shaped your self-esteem and self-image?

ASSIMILATING THE SHADOW: THERAPEUTIC PROCESS

Assimilating the shadow is a transformative process that leads to self-acceptance, forgiveness, and a shift from blame to responsibility. Therapeutic relationships, characterized by positive regard, understanding, and acceptance of shadow elements, provide a supportive environment for this integration.

How has self-acceptance and the integration of shadow elements positively impacted your personal growth, and what challenges have you encountered in this process?

THE THERAPIST'S SHADOW: MAINTAINING BALANCE

Therapists, too, have their own shadows, and maintaining balance is crucial to prevent potential distortions in the therapeutic relationship. The therapist's commitment to reliability, continuity, and compassion creates a space for the patient's shadow to be explored without judgment or rejection.

THE TRICKSTER AND THE WOLF: ARCHETYPAL SHADOWS

Archetypal figures like the Trickster and the Wolf symbolize collective shadows, encompassing both inferior and transformative traits. The Trickster, in particular, embodies qualities that can transcend evil and bring meaning to the seemingly meaningless.

Consider a period in your life when you encountered a situation or person embodying traits similar to the Trickster or the Wolf. This could be a friend, colleague, or even a personal challenge that brought about unexpected twists. Reflect on how navigating this experience contributed to your personal growth. How did you adapt to the unpredictability or challenges presented by this situation? In what ways did it prompt you to tap into transformative qualities within yourself, fostering resilience, creativity, or adaptability on your journey of personal development?

JUNG'S SHADOW: LEGACY AND EXPLORATION

Jung's own shadow elements, such as his anti-Semitism and idealization of the East, have left a legacy for those exploring his ideas. The shadowlands of organizations, while harboring potential for creativity, also pose challenges like splitting and projection.

WHY ENGAGE IN SHADOW WORK?

Shadow work is an incredible exploration of your inner self, with the ultimate destination being a place of profound self-acceptance and self-compassion. It's about knowing who you are, understanding the various facets that make up your being, and making peace with the thoughts and emotions that shape your actions. By acknowledging every part of yourself, even the shadowy aspects, you not only take charge of your life but also emerge as a more authentic and purposeful version of yourself.

The rewards of shadow work are numerous and extend to various aspects of your life, offering opportunities for personal growth such as:

- *Cultivating greater self-confidence and self-esteem*
- *Unleashing your enhanced creativity*
- *Strengthening your connections with others*
- *Nurturing self-acceptance*
- *Revealing hidden talents within you*
- *Breaking free from self-loathing*
- *Promoting overall well-being and reducing projection*
- *Fostering a heightened sense of empathy for those around you*

The beauty of shadow work lies in loving every part of yourself, even the darker corners. Remember that the shadow isn't inherently negative; it often harbors essential aspects of your personality that facilitate growth and positive transformation. Through shadow work, you unveil these latent strengths, reclaiming what may have been lost or forgotten. When you engage in self-reflection, a deeper understanding of yourself unfolds, leading to increased self-awareness and knowledge. With the practice of self-acceptance and self-love, your confidence and self-esteem blossom, paving the way for healthier relationships. Through shadow work, you may also uncover hidden talents and skills, opening doors to new opportunities for development and growth. When you engage in self-reflection, a deeper understanding of yourself unfolds, leading to increased self-awareness and knowledge. With the practice of self-acceptance and self-love, your confidence and self-esteem blossom, paving the way for healthier relationships. Through shadow work, you may also uncover hidden talents and skills, opening doors to new opportunities for development and growth.

UNDERSTANDING SHADOW WORK AND ITS PERSONAL IMPACT

Shadow work serves as a profound process that grants you insights into your true nature. It involves delving into your innermost thoughts, feelings, and emotions, and examining how they shape your behavior. Everyone possesses a shadow, whether it be fear, pain, anger, or something else entirely. The more you can integrate this shadow into your life, the healthier your overall well-being becomes. While shadow work is a potent tool for personal development, it's essential to note that it might not be suitable for everyone. If you're unsure, you can explore some shadow work prompts to gauge its resonance with you. If it feels challenging, it could be an indication that shadow work holds valuable benefits for you.

A PATH OF SELF-DISCOVERY

Initiating shadow work involves identifying your inner shadow, a crucial first step in this transformative journey. Pay attention to repeating patterns and habits in your life, both positive and negative, as they may hold clues to what is hindering or aiding you. Recognize any triggers that elicit reactions in you, as they can point to your shadow. Acknowledging and accepting your shadow enables you to unveil the truth of yourself, allowing you to show up authentically and honestly.

EXPLORATION OF YOUR SHADOW

While it may be a challenging process involving the exploration of negative thoughts and emotions, it's crucial to approach it with compassion and understanding. Make peace with yourself as you navigate through these aspects, appreciating the journey toward self-discovery.

HARNESSING THE MIRROR TECHNIQUE FOR SELF-EXPLORATION

During interactions with others, pay attention to your thoughts and feelings. If negativity surfaces, inquire if you are projecting. Reflect on your childhood and consider which emotions were deemed unacceptable—this can unveil insights into aspects of yourself labeled as "wrong" or "inferior."

CHOOSING COMPASSION OVER SHAME

Rather than succumbing to shame, practice self-compassion. Remind yourself of the inherent value you bring with affirming words such as "I trust in you," "I believe in you," "You are worthy of love," "You are enough," "You deserve to be happy," and "You have a lot to offer." When triggers bring forth emotions, observe them without judgment, allowing yourself to experience and process these feelings.

METHODS TO ILLUMINATE YOUR INNER WORLD

Shadow work can be approached through various methods. Maintaining a shadow journal offers a space to express both the dark and light aspects of yourself without censorship. Art therapy serves as a transformative means to process pre-verbal trauma and provide an outlet for your inner self. Engaging in a dialogue with your shadow, asking questions and listening without judgment, is another powerful method for self-discovery. Remember that this journey is uniquely yours, and the discoveries made along the way contribute to a more enriched and empowered version of yourself.

I understand that this journey can bring up various emotions and challenges, and I want you to know that practicing self-compassion is crucial if you want to discover the depths of your inner self. This book is here to assist you in navigating the process of shadow work, offering support as you uncover new aspects of yourself.

THOUGHTFUL QUESTIONS TO UNCOVER YOUR SHADOW SELF

Let's start this journey by considering some questions designed to illuminate your shadow self. These questions are not meant to overwhelm, but rather to gently guide you in self-reflection:

1. What is something about yourself that you wish others understood better?

....

....

....

2. Reflect on past instances when you might have told yourself untruths. What were they, and how did they shape your perspective?

....

....

....

3. Recollect a challenging memory from your childhood. How has this memory influenced the person you are today?

....

....

....

4. Consider both the positive and negative character traits of your parents. How do these traits manifest in your own life?

....

....

....

5. How do you react to drama, and what emotions does it stir within you?

....

....

....

6. Identify situations that make you feel self-conscious.

....

....

....

7. What circumstances create a sense of unease or insecurity for you?

....

....

....

8. Are you currently holding a grudge against someone, and if so, why?

....

....

....

9. Reflect on who has disappointed you the most in your life and the impact of that disappointment.

....

....

....

10. What actions or expressions make you feel valued by others?

....

....

....

11. Is there a quality in someone else that you admire but feel you lack? Why do you think you don't possess it?

....

....

....

12. Explore your core values and why they hold significance for you.

....

....

....

13. Consider your parent's core values during your childhood. How have these values evolved over time?

....

....

....

14. Recall instances when you've been particularly hard on yourself. What triggered this self-criticism?

....

....

....

15. Examine your relationship with failure. Does the concept make you anxious, and if so, why?

....

....

....

16. How do you cope with boredom, and what does it reveal about your inner self?

....

....

....

GUIDANCE FOR NAVIGATING SHADOW WORK

In addition to dedicating time for shadow work, remember to approach yourself with kindness and patience. I understand that shadow work can be challenging, but it is through this exploration that you build resilience and mental strength. If, at any point, you find that you need extra support, seeking professional guidance can be a beneficial step on your journey. Remember that you're not alone on this journey, and every step you take is a step toward a more authentic and fulfilled you.

Did you know that understanding your inner child is key to unlocking insights into your current behavior? The next chapter walks you through recognizing and comprehending your inner child, shedding light on its needs and its profound influence on your actions today.

CHAPTER 2:
MEETING YOUR INNER CHILD:
A KEY PLAYER
IN SHADOW WORK

> *The most sophisticated people I know*
> *- inside they are all children.*
>
> *– Jim Henson*

Have you ever thought about the little version of yourself that's been with you since the very beginning? From the early days in the womb to the tender years of being a baby, infant, toddler, and through middle school—our inner child has been there, soaking in both the good moments and the challenges.

Isn't it fascinating how this inner child of ours holds onto memories of joy and also those moments of fear, trauma, or loss from childhood? It's like our past experiences have left subtle imprints, creating a unique pattern within us. While it might be tricky to pinpoint the exact events causing these feelings, the beauty lies in recognizing the breadcrumb trails within our inner world. As we explore this internal landscape, we uncover a tapestry woven with both light and shadows, shaping the wonderful person we are today.

It's true for each of us—we all have an "inner child." That inner child of yours and mine is like a silent observer in our subconscious, absorbing messages long before it could fully grasp the mental and emotional nuances of the world around us. It carries a treasure trove of emotions, memories, and beliefs from our past, alongside the dreams and hopes that shape our future. Embracing and understanding this inner child is a beautiful journey that allows us to connect with the essence of who we are and the potential we hold within.

HOW DO WE TAP INTO OUR INNER CHILD?

Let's rewind to that comforting whiff of Grandma's embrace, her eyes gleaming with pride as we flaunted our bike-riding triumphs.

Our inner kid vividly recalls the heart-swelling joy when Dad gave us that approving look, a glint in his eyes, after sharing our prized toy with the neighbor.

Remember the thrill of getting invited to a friend's birthday bash? Confidence and happiness running high—those were the days.

Then there's the flip side. Our inner child holds onto the memory of tear-soaked cheeks when Mama rushed out to bid a hurried goodbye to her ailing dad.

Think back to the rough first day on the school bus, the awkwardness of being ignored—it's all part of our inner kid's baggage.

We've all been there, feeling a bit tongue-tied in class, catching the teacher's scoff, or drawing a blank on what seemed like an easy question.

Fast forward to landing that first job—the inner child stepping up, proving to the boss that we're not just goofing around.

In those teenage years, the inner kid is on a quest to fit in, craving love and finding their crew. It's about being understood and accepted.

But it's also the part that takes a hit when we're let down, ignored, or fed lies. The inner child feels the weight of betrayal and hurt, real and raw.

WHEN THE INNER CHILD TAKES CONTROL

Do you feel like something is preventing you from living your most fulfilled life?

When the inner child assumes control, one may observe the manifestation of emotions such as fear, perfectionism, anxiety, or a tendency to avoid specific people, places, or experiences. These responses serve as mechanisms through which the inner child endeavors to establish a sense of safety. When the inner child takes the lead, its behaviors, choices, and thoughts are influenced by unconscious beliefs or memories from the past, as well as the perceived necessities for the inner self to feel secure.

Frequently, the inner child lacks awareness of the current reality of the adult "self" and may remain oblivious to the changes in life. Emotional wounds from childhood can create a burden, akin to carrying a substantial weight on your back.

If the inner child is burdened with 50 pounds of pain, the sensation may parallel that of shouldering the weight of the world. If the inner child experienced instability, uncertainty, or danger, it could impede progress and deter you from making necessary changes. A fearful aspect may emerge, hindering your willingness to embrace new endeavors. Despite this fear, a desire to progress in life may generate a sense of internal conflict.

The impasse arises when one facet seeks safety and consistency while another seeks possibility, connection, and adventure. Resolving this dichotomy involves finding a middle ground to overcome stagnation. To foster a harmonious blend of creativity, flexibility, responsibility, connectivity, and consistency, it becomes imperative for your adult self and inner child to establish a connection. This initial step lays the foundation for a collaborative alliance, where the needs of both your adult self and inner child are acknowledged and addressed.

Picture yourself at the age of 5, immersed in the vibrant world of your kindergarten class. Laughter echoes on the playground as you play alongside your classmates. In the midst of the joy, a stumble sends you sprawling, and the once harmonious atmosphere takes a disheartening turn. The giggles of your peers pierce through the air, casting a shadow over your innocence.

The specifics of that moment may blur in your memory. The who, the where, the when—it's all a bit hazy. Yet, what lingers vividly is the overwhelming shame, the glistening tears that welled up, and the throbbing ache of your skinned knee. Perhaps you can even recall the solemn promise you made to yourself: "I won't let myself be ridiculed like that again."

Though the wound on your knee may have healed, the scars persist into adulthood. It's as if your inner 5-year-old, wounded and vulnerable, is still directing the show. Despite the passing of two or five decades, that inner child remains firmly in control. It's a struggle—you want to take risks, to seize opportunities, but the haunting echoes of the playground linger. The memory, even if faded, retains its grip on your present, dictating your actions and reactions.

Inner child work is like revisiting the pages of our own story, a journey into the heart of recognizing and healing the imprints left by our early struggles. It's a way of understanding that the way we navigate adulthood is often shaped by the footprints of our younger selves.

You see, it's about meeting the needs we might've missed back then, sort of like giving ourselves the care we wished we had received. In a way, it's becoming our own comforting companion, the one who understands our quirks, triggers, and the things that make our hearts sing.

So, when we dive into this inner child work, we're stepping into a vulnerable space, a place where we're both the grown-up and the little one who once faced the world wide-eyed. It's a bit like being a loving parent to ourselves, offering the kind of love, compassion, and support that can make all the difference. It's personal, it's conversational, and it's a journey back to our roots, where we can rediscover and embrace the essence of who we truly are.

WHAT CAUSES A WOUNDED INNER CHILD?

Think of your younger self as a little explorer navigating the landscape of life, encountering various situations that can leave lasting marks. Some wounds might seem small, like the disappointment of not getting a coveted toy. Others, however, cut deeper, etched by the shadows of physical abuse or the ache of emotional neglect.

It's like a collection of experiences, a scrapbook of moments both big and small, happy and painful. It's impossible to catalog every circumstance that your younger self internalized, but the echoes of those times often reverberate into your present. They shape the lens through which you view the world and influence the way you navigate your adult life.

Now, let's talk signs—little signals from your inner child that it might be carrying some wounds. Do you find yourself easily frustrated or irritated? Are your reactions sometimes disproportionate to the situation at hand? Picture those childish outbursts, the emotional storms where tantrums and words you didn't mean collided. Maybe there's a lingering complaint that no one truly understands you or hears your voice.

Expressing feelings becomes a puzzle, a tricky game of hide-and-seek with emotions. It's like you've got your own language, a struggle to explain why you feel the way you do (there's even a fancy term for it—alexithymia). And then there's the soundtrack of self-doubt, played by a particularly harsh inner critic.

Ever feel like there's a hint of immaturity, a pattern of self-sabotage dancing in the background? Perhaps there's a fear of abandonment or commitment issues, like your inner child is gripping onto the past. Setting boundaries or articulating needs becomes a bit of a challenge, and you wonder why.

If any of these patterns strike a chord, chances are those childhood wounds are still casting their shadows. Recognizing these signs is like turning on a light in the attic—you see what needs attention, what needs a bit of love and healing. It's a journey of understanding and embracing that little explorer within, offering the support and care that was missed along the way.

HOW IS INNER CHILD WORK LINKED TO SHADOW WORK?

Inner child work focuses on healing and understanding the wounded, vulnerable, and often neglected parts of ourselves that formed during childhood. The "inner child" represents the emotional and psychological residue of early life experiences, both positive and negative. Engaging in inner child work involves reconnecting with and nurturing this inner child to address unresolved issues, traumas, and unmet needs from the past. The goal is to foster healing, self-compassion, and personal growth by acknowledging and tending to the emotional wounds carried from childhood.

Shadow work, also rooted in Jungian psychology, deals with the unconscious or "shadow" aspects of the psyche. The shadow consists of repressed or denied feelings, desires, and traits that are often deemed unacceptable by societal norms or personal standards. Shadow work involves exploring and integrating these hidden aspects to achieve a more balanced and authentic self. It requires acknowledging and embracing the darker, less visible facets of one's personality, allowing for self-acceptance and a more comprehensive understanding of the self.

While inner child work focuses on the vulnerabilities developed in childhood, shadow work explores the deeper, hidden aspects of the adult psyche. Integrating these two approaches can be powerful because childhood experiences often contribute to the formation of the shadow. By addressing both the wounded inner child and the suppressed aspects of the shadow, individuals can achieve a more holistic understanding of themselves. This integrated approach facilitates healing, personal development, and a greater sense of wholeness.

We can't rewrite our history, but we can loosen the grip it has on us. Here are some down-to-earth ways to kickstart the healing process:

1. LISTEN TO YOURSELF

When frustration or emotional pain hits, pay attention. What's going on around you? Who are you talking to? Recognizing these triggers helps link them back to childhood wounds. Also, practice self-awareness through self-care. Meeting your own needs is a solid act of self-love.

2. MEDITATE

Meditation isn't just for yogis. It's a tool to sit with tough emotions. Learning to be present with your feelings is key for emotional regulation and stress management.

3. BUILD A NEW SET OF CAREGIVERS

Parents aren't perfect; growing up reveals that. Be your own parent now. When your inner wounded child surfaces, step in the way you wish someone had back then.

4. TRY INNER CHILD THERAPY

If you think you need professional support, there are therapists skilled in inner child work. They use various approaches, from shadow work to art therapy, helping you connect childhood experiences to adult behavior.

5. REIMAGINE YOUR CHILDHOOD

Guided meditations and visualization techniques help you connect with your younger self. Therapists trained in EMDR therapy can aid in recontextualizing past traumas, especially when PTSD is triggered.

6. TALK TO YOUR LOVED ONES

Grudges against family or childhood figures? Consider their perspective. A chat with a family member may reveal a side you never knew, fostering understanding and possibly repairing relationships.

7. REMEMBER HOW TO PLAY

Growing up shouldn't mean abandoning play. Rediscover the joy of taking chances and being creative. Ask yourself, "What would you do if others' opinions didn't matter?" Restoring your play muscle can bring back resilience and fearlessness.

8. CREATIVITY AND WORK

Inner child work not only heals emotional wounds but also rejuvenates your creativity. By freeing yourself from fear and self-consciousness, you become more innovative and resilient.

Are you feeling frustrated, angry, or stuck?

Your inner child might be calling for attention. Understanding how past experiences influence your present choices can bring clarity and purpose.

BENEFITS OF INNER CHILD WORK

1. ENHANCED SELF-AWARENESS

Inner child work fosters a deep understanding of your emotional landscape, allowing you to navigate your thoughts, feelings, and behaviors more consciously.

2. INSIGHT INTO PRESENT BEHAVIOR

Inner child work helps illuminate the roots of present behaviors, offering valuable insights into why certain patterns or reactions exist.

3. HEALTHY COPING MECHANISMS

The process encourages the development of healthier coping mechanisms, replacing outdated strategies with constructive ways of dealing with challenges.

4. RECONNECTION WITH PASSIONS AND DREAMS

Inner child work can reignite a connection with long-forgotten passions, dreams, and talents, allowing you to rediscover aspects of yourself that may have been set aside over the years.

5. EMPOWERMENT AND CONTROL

Through healing past wounds, inner child work empowers individuals, fostering a sense of control over their lives and choices.

6. IMPROVED EMOTIONAL REGULATION

Understanding and addressing the emotional imprints from childhood promotes improved emotional regulation, enabling more balanced responses to life's ups and downs.

7. INCREASED SELF-ESTEEM

As inner child work facilitates healing, it contributes to increased self-esteem by dismantling the negative self-perceptions rooted in past experiences.

8. HEIGHTENED SELF-COMPASSION

The process encourages self-compassion, allowing individuals to treat themselves with kindness and understanding, especially in moments of vulnerability or difficulty.

9. COMPASSION FOR OTHERS

When you learn to nurture and care for your inner child, there's a natural extension of compassion toward others, nurturing healthier relationships.

10. HOLISTIC PERSONAL AND PROFESSIONAL GROWTH

Inner child work, as part of mental fitness development, serves as a foundational element for comprehensive personal and professional growth, laying the groundwork for subsequent skills and achievements.

Imagine yourself as a diligent gardener, tending to the rich soil of your mind before planting the seeds of self-discovery. Just as every flourishing garden requires careful preparation, so does the garden of your inner world.

In the upcoming chapter, I'll be your guide, offering practical insights on crafting the perfect environment and mindset for your unique journey into shadow work. Get ready to cultivate the fertile ground within, as we explore together powerful and effective steps to ensure your personal growth takes root and flourishes. Your inner garden is waiting to bloom, and I'll be right there with you, nurturing the potential for a vibrant and thriving self. I know you too want to tap into your most authentic self.

CHAPTER 3:
SETTING THE STAGE
FOR SHADOW WORK

 *The shadow is needed now more than ever.*
We heal the world when we heal ourselves, and hope
shines brightest when it illuminates the dark.

– Sasha Graham

Did you know that natural survival instincts are designed to steer us away from pain, safeguarding our biological well-being?

When we experience pain, it signals a threat to our system, compelling us to address it promptly for the sake of our safety, health, and survival. The shadows that we carry can be particularly distressing, leading us to instinctively avoid confronting them at any cost.

The collective rejection of shadow traits by society reflects a broader dismissal of individuals who possess these traits. On a deeper level, we perceive society's rejection as a potential threat to our very existence. Without the support of our tribe, we may feel unattended, frail, and exposed, as if standing on the brink of a metaphorical demise. This underscores the profound significance of belonging—a crucial aspect of our well-being. Consequently, we often suppress these shadow traits, even though it comes at a personal and painful cost.

This pain stems from the act of denying oneself. By presenting only a one-sided image of goodness, we engage in a form of self-deception that leads to fragmentation and inauthenticity. The toll is exhausting, creating an unrealistic and unsustainable facade that ultimately takes a profound emotional toll.

WHY ENGAGE IN SHADOW WORK?

Engaging in shadow work may feel brutal, marked by discomfort, pain, and the unsettling revelation of aspects that may embarrass us. But do not fret, trust me that this journey is going to be worth it. The gains you achieve from learning the depths of your own darkness are invaluable, holding a treasure that can deeply impact your life in ways you may not even fathom.

The journey of shadow work leads to a sense of wholeness and freedom. It allows you to unearth deeper wells of love and compassion, both for yourself and others, creating a more profound connection with the world around you. Furthermore, this process enables you to make peace with yourself and those in your life.

Shadow work is a transformative path that brings an end to the incessant internal battles, paving the way for powerful and healing transformations. As you take on this journey, your capacity to experience true vitality increases, and both your inner and outer worlds undergo significant, positive changes. It's a challenging expedition, but the rewards are profound and far-reaching.

GRASPING THE ESSENCE OF NATURAL LAW

The world, as Joseph Campbell eloquently puts it, is both perfect and a bit of a mess—it always has been. Regardless of your personal beliefs, one undeniable truth persists: natural law is constantly unfolding within and around you.

Natural law isn't just an abstract concept; it's the very rhythm of our existence. It's evident in every breath, every laugh, every tear, and even in our moments of stumbling and messing up. It's the essence of who we are, and recognizing this is where the journey of shadow work begins.

Consider a drooling, pooping, crying baby. We don't harshly judge its inability to speak or use a toilet. Why? Because we understand that it's in the process of development, and that's perfectly okay.

Likewise, as adults, we throw tantrums, we scream, we make mistakes, we fall ill, and yes, sometimes we throw up. Why? Because we're human, and that's perfectly okay too.

This is nature at its core—unfiltered, untamed, and untaught in books. It's raw, pure, and undeniably true. This innate understanding of nature is what makes shadow work an incredibly potent and remarkable practice to change your current circumstances.

CREATING YOUR SAFE SPACE FOR SHADOW WORK

So, you're getting into the world of shadow work—think of it like prepping for a big project or committing to a major endeavor. It's like giving your own psyche a little makeover, a bit like renovating your house or going through a personal surgery. You wouldn't leave that kind of thing half-done, right? Just like a sudden storm or an unexpected challenge can mess up your house renovations, not fully committing to shadow work can cause some serious psychic chaos.

Here's a quick heads up to get you started. There's no breezy shortcut to shadow work. It's not a walk in the park, but that doesn't mean it's simple either. You can keep it straightforward, but it's not going to be a cakewalk. If you're not feeling those gut-wrenching, humbling depths, then you might need to switch gears.

Remember, if it feels easy, you might not be doing it right. So, are you ready to take the plunge? If the answer is yes, here are some effective methods to help you understand how to do shadow work:

1. CARVE OUT SACRED TIME FOR SELF-REFLECTION

Set aside a special evening devoted entirely to your personal growth journey. Embrace the warmth of self-discovery by gathering your thoughts on paper, in a journal, or on your computer. Cultivate a serene and secure environment for your introspection, perhaps in your room adorned with comforting elements like candles, incense, cozy blankets, and your favorite tea or water.

Craft a nurturing space because I understand that this process can be demanding. Take a few moments to reflect on aspects of yourself that you find challenging or have struggled to accept. Allow yourself to acknowledge these emotions with kindness and understanding.

2. BEGIN YOUR PRACTICE BY EMBRACING DEEP, INTENTIONAL BREATHS

Shadow work isn't always a lighthearted or effortless process. Acknowledging this challenge may make it tough to dedicate time to introspection. Ease into the process by grounding yourself through deliberate breathing exercises. This not only creates a sense of presence but also brings a calming influence to your mind, body, and spirit, making the journey more approachable.

3. TAKE A MOMENT TO GAIN SOME PERSPECTIVE ON YOUR LIFE

Picture yourself as an observer, an onlooker in your own life. Consider how a friend might perceive you and respond to your actions and behaviors in different situations. By addressing these inquiries, you can unveil recurring behavioral patterns and emotions.

Pay attention to the recurring ways you respond to specific words, situations, or events.

Pose reflective questions like, "Why did that affect me? What prompted that emotion or behavior?"

Cap off your day with a combination of meditation and journaling to sift through your thoughts, process your experiences, and reflect on your actions. This practice helps create self-awareness and understanding.

4. EMBRACE SELF-HONESTY ON YOUR HEALING JOURNEY

Acknowledging that healing is a gradual process, it's essential to recognize that true progress unfolds when you're completely honest with yourself. We understand that unveiling your less favorable traits can be challenging, but it's a step toward personal growth. Even if the truth is tough to accept, it serves as a valuable lesson, guiding you toward evolving into the best version of yourself.

5. CHALLENGE YOUR IMMEDIATE REACTIONS

Take a moment to pause, reflect, and delve into the reasons behind your emotions before reacting impulsively. If you sense judgment or a negative comment arising, resist the urge and ask yourself, "What prompted this reaction? Why was I inclined to say that?" By interrupting the automatic response and allowing space for reflection, you pave the way for reframing your thoughts and actions toward a more positive direction.

6. RECOGNIZE, COMPREHEND, AND GRANT YOURSELF COMPASSION FOR YOUR INSECURITIES

Now that you've brought to light aspects of your personality that may have cast a shadow on your life, it's crucial to create room for self-forgiveness and growth. Life is a journey of constant transformation, and it's natural to evolve along with it. However, it's perfectly acceptable to question these changes. As you undergo this process, acknowledge the aspects of yourself that you wish to improve, seek to understand the reasons behind shifts in your thinking, and extend forgiveness to yourself.

Remember that this isn't an overnight transformation, and that's absolutely okay. Progress at your own pace, gradually exploring new facets of your shadow when you feel ready. Healing is a patient journey, so approach it with kindness and gentleness toward yourself.

7. EXPLORE THE THERAPEUTIC BENEFITS OF ART

Engaging in activities like doodling, painting, dancing, or singing provides expressive and artistic avenues to connect with your shadow. Choose a medium that resonates with you, whether it's oil paints or modern dance, and allow your emotions and creativity to flow freely. This artistic expression can serve as a powerful tool to bring forth repressed feelings and images, creating a space for deeper analysis and understanding.

8. CONSIDER CONSULTING A THERAPIST SKILLED IN SHADOW WORK

Certain therapists and psychologists specialize in guiding individuals through the process of shadow work. They may use techniques such as creating a meditative state to facilitate exploration of the deepest aspects of your shadow, asking probing questions to access repressed memories, and analyzing projections.

If you're considering professional assistance for shadow work, it's important to inquire about the therapist's specific training in this area before scheduling an appointment. This ensures that you receive tailored support and guidance in navigating the complexities of your shadow self.

9. COMPOSE A HEARTFELT LETTER TO YOUR SHADOW

Inscribe your genuine feelings about it with pen and paper. Reflect on whether it has brought you pain or if there's a part of you that envies its traits. Be open and honest—there's no prescribed "right" or "wrong" way to express yourself. Once you've poured out your sentiments onto the paper, consider tearing it up, tossing it into a fire, or crumpling it into a ball. This symbolic act serves as a powerful means to release any lingering resentment while acknowledging the complex relationship that you share with your shadow.

10. PRACTICE SAYING DAILY AFFIRMATIONS TO EMPOWER YOURSELF

Harness the transformative potential by reshaping the narrative around your shadow. Reflect on aspects of yourself that you find challenging and contemplate how they impact you negatively. Then, craft positive affirmations to reframe these traits. For instance, if you often criticize your body, shift your focus to the affirmation, "I love my body for all it does for me." Consider incorporating these affirmations into your daily routine:

1. I am deserving of love, affection, and respect.
2. I am powerful, strong, and courageous.
3. I honor and love my shadow, embracing all parts of myself.
4. I speak my truth, even when it's difficult.
5. I deserve love and respect, even in my lowest moments.

Repeat these affirmations regularly to instill a positive mindset and cultivate self-compassion.

HEALING IS A PROCESS

Within each of us resides inner struggles, battles against our own demons—a daily confrontation with outcomes that vary between victory and defeat.

These internal demons manifest themselves in subtle glimpses or overwhelming chaos, shadows that, due to guilt and shame, we often prefer to disregard and bury deep within ourselves. Society encourages us to emphasize the positive aspects of our existence—love and light—while dismissing the darkness or shadow that coexists within.

Concentrating solely on the positive side is undeniably easy and comforting. It's understandable why many of us shy away from delving into the darker corners of our personalities.

Yet, when our focus remains fixated on the "light," it barely scratches the surface of our being. It feels akin to holding onto something warm and fuzzy.

> *Positive thinking is simply the philosophy of hypocrisy – to give it the right name. When you are feeling like crying, it teaches you to sing. You can manage if you try, but those repressed tears will come out at some point, in some situation. There is a limitation to repression. And the song that you were singing was absolutely meaningless; you were not feeling it, it was not born out of your heart*
>
> **– Osho**

Here's what you can do to conquer your shadow self and own your life as It was meant to be lived:

STEP 1: KNOW YOUR WORTH AND BELIEVE IN POSITIVE CHANGE

To reclaim control over your life and confront your shadow self, the foundational step is acknowledging your inherent worthiness of positive experiences.

During moments of low spirits, it's natural to perpetuate those feelings. Humans possess a unique talent for self-pity, and at times, it serves a purpose. However, when self-pity becomes all-encompassing, breaking free from that cycle and returning to normal routines, or better yet, our best selves, can prove challenging.

The crux lies in cultivating self-love.

Yet, practicing self-love in today's societal context can be challenging.

Why?

Because societal norms often dictate that our sense of self is intertwined with our relationships. The prevailing notion is that true happiness and fulfillment come from finding love with another person.

As famous Shaman Rudá landê said: "If you do not respect your whole, you cannot expect to be respected as well. Don't let your partner love a lie, an expectation. Trust yourself. Bet on yourself. If you do this, you will be opening yourself to be really loved. It's the only way to find real, solid love in your life."

STEP 2: UNVEILING THE SHADOW

Our shadows, deeply entrenched within our subconscious, are intentionally concealed, making identification a nuanced endeavor.

The initial stride is to heighten awareness of the persistent emotions that weave through your experiences. This heightened consciousness serves as a spotlight, illuminating the contours of your shadow.

Common shadow beliefs that may surface include:

1. I am not good enough.
2. I am unlovable.
3. I am flawed.
4. My feelings are not valid.
5. I must take care of everyone around me.
6. Why can't I just be normal, like others?

By acknowledging these recurring sentiments, you initiate a process of recognition that lays the groundwork for shadow work—an exploration that holds the promise of profound self-discovery and growth.

STEP 3: EXAMINE YOUR FEELINGS WITH OBJECTIVITY AND COMPASSION

Conducting shadow work with objectivity and compassion poses a challenge, as it is often more convenient to investigate and assign blame to external factors for our current state.

Conversely, comprehending the motivations behind the actions of those who may have caused us pain is a difficult task. Yet, for our own healing journey, it is imperative to cultivate forgiveness toward those who have hurt us, enabling us to progress.

Experiencing negative emotions is an intrinsic aspect of being human, and there's no need to harbor guilt for such feelings. Recognizing that everyone encounters these sentiments is a fundamental acknowledgment of our shared humanity.

It holds paramount significance to accept these negative emotions without judgment. Philosopher Alan Watts and Carl Jung both exemplify individuals who could confront negativity without shame, emphasizing the importance of allowing ourselves the space to experience and understand our emotions. This acceptance becomes a powerful cornerstone in the process of self-discovery and emotional well-being.

STEP 4: EXPLORE THE DEPTHS OF YOUR SHADOW SELF

Psychologists often utilize art therapy as a means for patients to delve into their inner selves, recognizing that art provides a powerful avenue for the manifestation of the Shadow. Here are various ways to express and explore your shadow self:

1. JOURNALING

Writing allows emotions to surface and unburden the mind of swirling thoughts. It's a liberating process where even seemingly nonsensical thoughts find a place on paper. There's no right or wrong way; just let the words flow.

2. WRITE A LETTER

Pen a letter to yourself or those who've caused you pain. This therapeutic exercise need not be sent; its purpose is to release pent-up emotions. Express your feelings and rationale behind them. Consider burning the letter symbolically for a cathartic release.

3. MEDITATION

Meditation unveils insights into our emotions, fostering understanding and objective exploration. Practices like forgiveness meditation, where you wish well for those who hurt you, can be transformative.

4. FEEL

Confronting and expressing the emotions you fear is essential for healing. Write about them, create art, and allow yourself to experience the full spectrum of emotions to truly embrace your wholeness.

5. DREAMS

According to Jung, dreams can unveil our deepest thoughts and emotions: "The dream is the small hidden door in the deepest and most intimate sanctum of the soul, which opens to that primeval cosmic night that was soul long before there was conscious ego and will be soul far beyond what a conscious ego could ever reach." Document your dreams immediately upon waking to gain insights into your subconscious and further understand yourself.

The shadow thrives in secrecy but is an integral part of who you are. Illuminate the concealed aspects of yourself with self-love and acceptance, even if the process is challenging. Keep in mind:

- *To attain your desires, confront and embrace your inner darkness.*
- *Rather than suppressing the shadow self, allow yourself to feel and be curious about it.*
- *In some instances, the shadow can serve you, especially in protecting your higher self.*
- *When tapped into properly, the shadow self can be a potent ally in managing challenging situations.*
- *Problems arise when the shadow rules your life or is denied, rather than acknowledged.*

STEP 5: CARING FOR YOUR INNER CHILD

Childhood traumas, stemming from parenting or experiences of harm by others, often create deep wounds that shape behavioral and emotional patterns, molding our personalities.

Frequently, it is our childhood wounds that are the most poignant, echoing messages that we are unworthy of love, our feelings are invalid, or that we must shoulder all responsibilities due to a lack of care.

Nurturing your inner child involves a journey back in time to moments of vulnerability, providing yourself with the love you needed. Here's how:

REVISIT VULNERABLE MOMENTS

Transport yourself to a time when you felt most vulnerable. Hold that image in your mind, staying attuned to any emerging messages from that period.

OFFER COMPASSION

While revisiting those moments, extend love and compassion to your younger self. Speak words of reassurance, saying, "I love you, I'm here for you. It will be okay; it's not your fault, and you did nothing to deserve this." Consider even giving a symbolic hug to your younger self.

Confronting flaws, weaknesses, selfishness, hatred, and other negative emotions is a challenging process. However, while focusing on our positive aspects boosts confidence, shadow work facilitates personal growth, guiding us toward a more authentic and fulfilling life.

As Jung expressed in his book Psychology and Alchemy: "There is no light without shadow and no psychic wholeness without imperfection." Through shadow work, we embark on a journey toward completeness, enabling us to lead a more genuine and enriching life.

Ever feel like you're on a self-discovery journey, but distractions and overwhelm keep pulling you away? Imagine you're exploring your shadow self, and suddenly, life's chaos tries to take over. Grounding techniques could be your secret weapon to stay centered and focused during moments like these. Head to the next chapter to find out more.

CHAPTER 4:

PLANTING YOUR FEET:
GROUNDING TECHNIQUES

Ever since life started moving at a seemingly relentless pace, I've often found myself yearning for a way to hit the pause button, if only for a moment. It's in those hectic stretches, whether facing a barrage of deadlines or navigating the challenges of daily life, that I stumbled upon the concept of grounding.

Grounding became my sanctuary, a mindful retreat within the chaos. From the gentle grip of soil beneath my feet to the rhythmic flow of controlled breaths, grounding has become my compass, helping me find solace in the present moment. It's not just a technique for me; it's more like a lifeline.

WHAT IS GROUNDING?

Connecting with Earth, often referred to as grounding or earthing, involves a practice where individuals establish a link between their physical bodies and the electrical energy of Earth. Our planet carries a negative electric charge, and some scientists propose that grounding facilitates the transfer of free electrons to the human body.

This electrical connection can potentially bring about several positive physical outcomes, such as alleviating pain, influencing immune responses, promoting wound healing, impacting inflammation, and even contributing to the potential prevention and management of autoimmune diseases and chronic inflammatory conditions.

Numerous individuals share experiences highlighting the spiritual dimensions of grounding, expressing a sense of peace, heightened meditation, and contentment following a grounding session. Frequently, grounding is viewed as a means to establish a connection with Mother Earth or a larger force, allowing individuals to internally revert to a simpler way of life characterized by a more harmonious rhythm with our planet.

Grounding, also known as earthing, might seem unconventional to many. For those intrigued, the question of how to ground oneself may arise. Fortunately, there are various ways to engage in grounding practices.

Grounding exercises can be as simple as standing or walking barefoot, or pressing your uncovered hands into the grass or soil. However, in the context of modern Western society, going barefoot outdoors is not always feasible, except perhaps at the beach. To address this, grounding tools have been developed to replicate the electrical conduction of biological grounding. These tools include specialized items such as mats, wrist or ankle bands, sheets, adhesive patches, and even footwear.

For these tools to be effective, they are typically connected to the ground through a cord linked to a grounded electrical wall outlet or a rod directly pressed into the soil. This innovative approach allows individuals to experience the benefits of grounding even in environments where going barefoot may not be practical.

Finding ways to ground yourself outdoors involves establishing a direct electrical connection with Earth, aiming to reestablish a link often lost in our contemporary, industrially driven society where shoes with rubber soles and indoor living predominate.

To practice grounding outdoors effectively, it's essential to allow your bare skin to directly touch the ground. This involves the simple act of removing your shoes and socks. Here are various ways to engage in grounding outdoors:

1. *Walk barefoot on dirt, grass, or sand regularly.*
2. *Stand with bare feet on humid dirt or sand.*
3. *Press your bare hands into the grass or earth.*
4. *Sit on a chair, bench, or wheelchair with your bare feet flat on the ground.*
5. *Lie flat on dirt, grass, sand, or gravel with exposed back, legs, or arms.*
6. *Immerse yourself in a natural body of water, such as swimming in a pond, lake, or ocean.*
7. *Engage in gardening with your bare hands in the soil.*

If you have a yard, you may choose to practice earthing in the comfort of your own space. Alternatively, you can explore public parks, woodland trails, or enjoy a barefoot stroll on a beach. Some countries even have designated barefoot parks. If the idea of walking in public without shoes makes you uncomfortable, consider bringing a small bag to store your shoes after walking to a secluded spot where you can comfortably remove them.

Grounding can also be incorporated into indoor settings through the use of specialized tools. While it's true that some of these tools come with associated costs, they offer a convenient alternative to walking barefoot, making grounding practices more accessible for some individuals. These tools can be worn discreetly inside shoes, on the ankles or wrists throughout the day, or even utilized during sleep, facilitating a consistent and convenient grounding routine.

TYPES OF GROUNDING?

Grounding or earthing encompasses various methods, all centered around the idea of reconnecting with Earth. These approaches involve either direct or indirect contact with Earth's surface. Here are some types of grounding:

WALKING BAREFOOT

This simple and natural practice involves walking barefoot on surfaces such as grass, sand, or mud. Direct skin-to-earth contact during this activity allows for a grounding energy exchange.

LYING ON THE GROUND

Increase your connection by lying directly on the ground, whether it's the grass in a park or the sandy shores of a beach. However, always ensure you choose a safe location to avoid potential harm.

SUBMERSING IN WATER

Advocates of grounding suggest that water can be used similarly to the earth for grounding. Activities like wading in a clear lake or swimming in the ocean are considered ways to ground yourself. Exercise caution, especially in unfamiliar or deep waters.

USING GROUNDING EQUIPMENT

For situations where outdoor grounding is impractical, various grounding tools offer alternatives. One method involves connecting a metal rod to the ground outside and linking it to your body through a wire. Alternatively, there are specific grounding equipment options designed for indoor use, making earthing therapy accessible in daily life. These include:

- Grounding mats
- Grounding sheets or blankets
- Grounding socks
- Grounding bands and patches

These tools provide effective ways to incorporate grounding practices into your routine, offering flexibility and convenience when outdoor grounding is not feasible.

Discovering the neglected parts of yourself, the ones you've pushed away and hidden in the depths of your unconscious, is what shadow work is all about. It might seem easier to keep those aspects at a distance, tied up and tossed aside. However, these rejected fragments could hold the key to unlocking a healthier, more complete, and successful version of yourself.

Embracing shadow work involves bringing these overlooked pieces back into your conscious awareness, a process known as shadow integration. It's a profound healing practice that can transform these once-dismissed fragments into the stars of your personal growth journey. The shadow often conceals genuine gifts and untapped potential, and by integrating them, you open doors to unexpected avenues of personal development.

Yet, it's crucial to acknowledge that this journey can be challenging and at times painful. It requires courage and resilience, but the rewards are immeasurable. However, before embarking on the transformative path of shadow work, it's essential to establish a foundation through grounding.

And, if you stay with me until the end, I'll share a quick and effective grounding technique to support you on this profound journey.

Here are five compelling reasons why grounding is a prerequisite:

1. SHADOW WORK CAN BRING UP INTENSE EMOTIONS

Engaging in shadow work may stir up strong emotions as you explore the less appealing aspects of yourself—those parts that may evoke feelings of jealousy, manipulation, anger, greed, lust, and more. It's a journey that can sometimes feel like navigating chaos and losing control. In these moments, connecting with the grounding energy of the earth becomes crucial, offering a stabilizing force that is incredibly valuable during this powerful healing process.

2. EMBODIED HEALING: GROUNDING AS THE FOUNDATION FOR EMPOWERING SHADOW WORK

Grounding serves as a way to connect with your own physical presence, and this connection becomes especially vital when delving into the depths of shadow work. Shadow work has a way of challenging the essence of who you are, unraveling the layers of an identity formed through years of concealing, suppressing, and denying aspects of yourself. As these familiar patterns are untangled, it's natural to feel a sense of uncertainty about the person you once believed yourself to be.

Amidst this uncertainty, there's solace in the constancy of your body.

Your body is your haven, a place of belonging, and it offers a dependable anchor. While the journey of shadow work may shake the foundations of your identity, the reassuring presence of your physical self remains a steadfast companion throughout.

3. SHADOW WORK MAY FEEL UNSAFE

When you engage yourself in shadow work it might stir feelings of unease, as it involves peeling back layers of self-perception. The process of profound healing dismantles the identity you once believed defined you, creating a sense of insecurity as the familiar "you" fades away.

Nevertheless, the body tends to be a secure and known refuge for many. Establishing a connection with it through grounding practices acts as a stabilizing link to the concept of home.

4. NURTURING PRESENCE THROUGH GROUNDING

As you step into the world of shadow work, exploring far-off realms—diving into the depths of your past, exploring sideways into different realities, and reaching forward into what could be. But here's the thing: shadow work can make you feel a bit unmoored, like you're floating away! That's why it's so crucial to ground yourself before you dive in, so that you don't end up feeling totally adrift. Let's make sure that you're anchored before taking this path further.

5. BRIDGING OUR CONNECTION TO MOTHER EARTH

Picture Earth as our timeless, archetypal mother—the ultimate creatrix guiding us through every phase and cycle of personal growth. When we ground ourselves and forge a connection with her, it's like creating an unbreakable cord of safety, nurture, and support that surpasses our individual strength.

By energetically linking to Mother Earth, you anchor yourself in her profound, nurturing wisdom. This not only shapes your shadow work journey into something archetypal but transforms the healing process into a collective benefit. Your efforts extend beyond personal growth; they become a healing dance with and for the collective, as Mother Earth senses and resonates with the transformative energy of your shadow work.

JUST LIKE I PROMISED HERE'S A SIMPLE GROUNDING RITUAL TO IGNITE YOUR SHADOW WORK (AND SAFEGUARD YOUR JOURNEY)

◆ Close your eyes and tune into your breath.

◆ Take a few unhurried, deep breaths to calm your nervous system, letting the rhythm find its natural pace.

◆ Envision a cherished spot in nature. It could be a familiar haunt, a one-time visit, or even a place captured in a photograph or movie. Immerse yourself in the details—see, hear, feel, and smell everything about this beautiful location, tapping into the strength of your imagination.

◆ Now, sense the love you hold for this place. Let it gather in your heart (if challenging, draw upon the emotions for something else you love—a child, a pet, your partner, or any other source of affection).

◆ Allow this love to expand in your heart, radiating like pulsating light.

◆ Once your love feels potent, use your will and imagination to compress it into a small ball. Drop it down from your heart, through your body, and into Earth's core. Picture it descending, releasing the love as it goes.

◆ Pause. Something extraordinary often unfolds next, and you're likely to feel it.

◆ Open your senses to Earth reciprocating with her love. Experience it rising gently from below, activating a subtle flow through your body.

◆ As your love for Earth may resurge, gently guide it downward again, creating a continuous loop between you and the planet, allowing love to circulate freely.

◆ Revel in this sensation for as long as you desire.

Now, let the journey into shadow work begin!

In the fast-paced rhythm of our daily lives, finding a moment of calm and connection can be transformative. Join me as we explore a collection of fabulous grounding techniques, each designed to anchor your mind, soothe your spirit, and foster a profound sense of serenity. Whether you're seeking relief from stress or simply aiming to enhance your mindfulness practice, these techniques are sure to become invaluable tools on your path to a more centered and harmonious life.

POWERFUL GROUNDING TECHNIQUES

Let me paint a scene that might feel all too familiar. It's a Wednesday evening, and the day has been a rollercoaster of work, family obligations, and unexpected challenges. As you finally sink into your favorite chair, there's this lingering stress, a buzzing in your mind that refuses to quiet down.

Maybe it's the weight of deadlines or the echoes of a tough conversation. In these moments, grounding techniques become a lifeline. Picture being able to take a breath, to consciously step back from the chaos, and find a moment of peace within yourself. It's not about escaping reality but about reclaiming your center in life.

These grounding techniques are the secret sauce to turning those frazzled evenings into moments of self-care and resilience, where you're not just surviving but thriving in the midst of it all.

Explore these grounding techniques that leverage your senses and tangible objects to guide you through moments of distress:

PHYSICAL GROUNDING TECHNIQUES

IMMERSE YOUR HANDS IN WATER

Concentrate on the water's temperature and its sensation on your fingertips, palms, and the backs of your hands. Is the experience consistent across all parts of your hand? Experiment with warm water followed by cold, and vice versa, noting any differences in sensation.

ENGAGE WITH NEARBY OBJECTS

Feel the textures, weights, and temperatures of items within reach. Focus on the nuanced details, challenging yourself to describe colors in vivid terms like crimson, burgundy, indigo, or turquoise instead of using generic labels like red or blue.

PRACTICE DEEP BREATHING

Inhale and exhale slowly, vocalizing or thinking "in" and "out" with each breath. Be attuned to the filling and release of air in your lungs.

INDULGE IN A FOOD OR DRINK

Take deliberate, small bites or sips of something you enjoy. Allow yourself to fully experience the taste, aroma, and lingering flavors on your tongue.

EMBARK ON A BRIEF WALK

Pay attention to each step, even counting them if it helps. Notice the rhythm of your footsteps: and the feeling of your foot making contact with the ground.

HOLD AN ICE CUBE

Explore the initial sensations and observe how they change as the ice begins to melt. Take note of the evolving experience.

APPRECIATE A SCENT

Inhale the fragrance of something appealing, be it tea, an herb, a favorite soap, or a scented candle. Concentrate on the scent's qualities, such as sweetness, spiciness, or citrusy notes.

MOVE YOUR BODY

Partake in exercises or stretches like jumping jacks, bouncing, jumping rope, jogging in place, or targeting different muscle groups individually. Observe the sensations in your body with each movement, including how your hands or feet interact with the floor or air.

LISTEN TO YOUR SURROUNDINGS

Take a moment to identify the sounds around you—birds, dogs, machinery, or traffic. If people are talking, try to understand the conversation or recognize the language. Let these sounds ground you in your present location.

TUNE INTO YOUR BODY

Whether seated or standing, focus on each part of your body, considering details such as hair on your shoulders, the weight of your shirt, and the sensation in your arms and legs. Pay attention to your heartbeat, stomach fullness, and the position of your legs and feet.

EXPERIMENT WITH THE 5-4-3-2-1 METHOD

Engage in the 5-4-3-2-1 method to heighten your awareness of the present moment. Start from 5, using your senses to identify and appreciate the details around you:

5 things you hear
4 things you see
3 things you can touch from your current position
2 things you can smell
1 thing you can taste

Challenge yourself to observe the often-overlooked nuances, like the subtle color variations in the carpet flecks or the gentle hum emanating from your computer. This practice fosters a mindful connection with your surroundings and encourages you to savor the richness of your immediate environment.

MENTAL GROUNDING TECHNIQUES

Explore these mental grounding techniques to divert your thoughts from distressing feelings and reconnect with the present moment:

ENGAGE IN A MEMORY GAME

Briefly study a detailed photograph or picture for 5–10 seconds, then turn it face-down. Recreate the image in your mind, focusing on intricate details. Alternatively, mentally list all the elements you recall from the picture.

CATEGORIZE YOUR THOUGHTS

Choose broad categories like "musical instruments," "ice cream flavors," or "baseball teams." Take a minute to mentally list as many items as possible within each category.

UTILIZE MATH AND NUMBERS

Even if math isn't your forte, numbers can be grounding. Try running through a times table, counting backward from 100, or thinking of five ways to make a chosen number.

RECITE FAMILIAR CONTENT

Recall a poem, song, or book passage from memory. Recite it quietly to yourself, paying attention to the shape of each word if spoken aloud, or visualize the words as they appear on a page if recited mentally.

INDUCE LAUGHTER

Create a lighthearted joke or enjoy a funny video. Engage with content that brings a smile to your face and lightens the mood

USE AN ANCHORING STATEMENT

Craft a statement that anchors you in the present moment, including details about yourself, the date, time, and your current surroundings. Expand on the details until you feel a sense of calm.

ENVISION A DAILY TASK YOU ENJOY

Imagine performing a routine task you find pleasant, like putting away freshly laundered clothes. Focus on the sensory details and steps involved to enhance the visualization.

DESCRIBE A FAMILIAR TASK

Select a task you frequently perform or excel at, such as making coffee or locking up your office. Walk through the steps as if you are giving instructions to someone else.

PICTURE LEAVING PAINFUL FEELINGS BEHIND

Visualize gathering negative emotions, placing them in a box, and distancing yourself from them through activities like walking, swimming, or cycling. Imagine your distressing thoughts as a song or TV show and change the channel or lower the volume.

OBSERVE AND DESCRIBE YOUR SURROUNDINGS

Take a few minutes to absorb your environment, using all five senses to provide detailed descriptions. Engage with your surroundings, noting colors, textures, temperatures, and sounds to ground yourself in the present experience.

Did you know that grounding through breathwork goes beyond just a mental exercise?

It's intriguing to discover that practices like diaphragmatic or belly breathing have a real impact on our physiology. When we engage in intentional and deep breathing, we're actually triggering the parasympathetic nervous system—the "rest and digest" system. This not only leads to a noticeable reduction in cortisol, the stress hormone, but also promotes a heightened sense of relaxation (Jerath et al., 2006).

We do it many, many times a day—and yet how many of us are really conscious of the true power of the breath?

Breathwork is fundamentally the deliberate utilization of the breath. In essence, it involves learning to control the rhythm of breathing to achieve equilibrium in both the body and mind. Additionally, breathwork can be viewed as a variant of active meditation. The International Breathwork Foundation (IBF) characterizes this practice as "a dynamic body-mind practice using conscious connected breathing techniques for inner peace, enhanced health, wellbeing and personal transformation." Breathwork comprises diverse therapeutic methods and exercises aimed at alleviating mental, physical, and emotional stress.

The advantages of incorporating breathwork into your routine are substantial, particularly in counteracting the effects of the "fight-or-flight" response triggered by stress. This physiological reaction, marked by the release of hormones like cortisol and adrenaline, can lead to increased breathing rates, elevated pulse and blood pressure, and a state of heightened alertness.

Here are four key benefits of maintaining a consistent breathwork practice:

IMMEDIATE RELIEF

Breathwork offers swift relief by inducing changes in your physiology almost instantly. Adjusting the patterns of your inhalation, exhalation, and breath holds empowers you to shift from a stress-induced sympathetic response to a more calming parasympathetic state.

LOW LEARNING CURVE

Mastering breathwork requires minimal learning. Since you're already breathing, the key is to alter the ratios in which you breathe. Accessible techniques make it easy for anyone to integrate breathwork into their routine.

VERSATILITY IN APPLICATION

Breathwork is a portable practice that can be done inconspicuously anywhere, whether you're on a bus or at work. Adjusting your breath throughout the day allows you to regulate your response to daily fluctuations and challenges.

DIVERSE BENEFITS

Establishing a regular breathwork practice provides a universal tool with multiple advantages. It helps alleviate anxiety, boost immune function, enhance focus, and improve athletic performance.

While the benefits are significant, it's important to acknowledge potential challenges for those new to breathwork:

INITIAL DISCOMFORT

Changing physiology may generate unfamiliar sensations due to shifts in blood chemistry. For newcomers, this can feel strange initially.

REQUIRES DEDICATION

Like any skill, realizing the full benefits of breathwork demands commitment and consistent practice.

BUILDING CONFIDENCE

Gaining confidence in the knowledge that you have control over your breath is crucial. The practice builds resilience, making the perceived threat of being out of breath less intimidating over time.

THREE BREATH WORK EXERCISES YOU CAN TRY TO GROUND YOURSELF

Explore these mental grounding techniques to divert your thoughts from distressing feelings and reconnect with the present moment:

EXERCISE 1: 4–7–8 TECHNIQUE

The 4–7–8 breathing exercise stands out for its simplicity, efficiency, and accessibility. Requiring no special equipment and adaptable to any setting, this exercise can be seamlessly integrated into your routine. While it can be done in any position, it is recommended to sit with a straight back during initial practice. Position the tip of your tongue against the ridge of tissue just behind your upper front teeth, maintaining this placement throughout the exercise.

WHEN TO USE IT

Once you cultivate this breathing technique through daily, twice-a-day practice, it becomes a valuable resource that you can carry with you always. Apply it whenever faced with upsetting situations, providing a moment to center yourself before reacting. Use it to address internal tension, facilitate sleep, or manage food cravings. Particularly effective for mild to moderate anxiety, this exercise comes highly recommended.

HOW TO DO IT

1. Exhale completely through your nose.
2. Close your mouth and inhale quietly through your nose, counting mentally to four.
3. Hold your breath for a count of seven.
4. Exhale completely through your nose, counting to eight.
5. One complete breath cycle. Inhale again and repeat the sequence three more times, totaling four breaths.

EXERCISE 2: BOX BREATHING

Box breathing, also recognized as square breathing, serves as a technique for engaging in deliberate, slow, and deep breaths. This method proves effective in enhancing performance, fostering concentration, and acting as a potent stress reliever.

WHEN TO USE IT

Box breathing offers benefits to individuals seeking meditation or stress reduction. Consider integrating it into your routine before interviews, significant work pitches, challenging conversations, or during moments of traffic-induced stress.

HOW TO DO IT

1. Prior to starting, ensure you are seated upright in a comfortable chair with feet flat on the floor. Keep your hands relaxed in your lap, palms facing up, and focus on maintaining proper posture—sitting up straight to facilitate deep breaths.

2. Sit upright and exhale slowly through your nose until your lungs are empty, focusing on this intentional action.

3. Inhale slowly and deeply through your nose, counting to five. Feel the air fill your lungs gradually, section by section, until your lungs are completely full, and the air reaches your abdomen.

4. Hold your breath for a count of five seconds, maintaining a relaxed body with a mild "lock" in your throat area.

5. Exhale evenly for a count of five seconds.

6. Hold all air out of your empty lungs for a count of five seconds—a phase often experienced as surprisingly peaceful.

7. Repeat this cycle until you feel content, aiming for at least five rounds.

EXERCISE 3: RESONANCE

Resonant breathing serves as a transformative practice, offering a reclaiming of your authentic self and reinstating control in the face of life's increasing demands. This technique invites you to dedicate a few minutes each day to live and breathe in a state of perfect balance between the sympathetic and parasympathetic nervous systems—an oasis of mental calm, equilibrium, and conscious peace.

The Breathing App, available on Apple and Android platforms, was conceptualized by Eddie Stern, a respected yoga teacher, author, and lecturer from New York. Inspired by resonance, a scientific phenomenon where heart rate, heart rate variability, blood pressure, and brainwave function synchronize into a coherent frequency, this app mirrors the natural breathing rhythm of Buddhist monks and Yogis, occurring at a rate of six breaths per minute during meditation.

HOW TO DO IT

Choose from four breath ratios by determining the duration of your inhale through a slow, slightly elongated inhalation. The inhale length automatically sets the exhale duration. The exception is a five-second inhale, which allows for either a five or seven-second exhale. Opt for the longer exhale for a more engaging response from the parasympathetic nervous system.

THE RATIOS ARE

1. Inhale for four seconds, exhale for six seconds
2. Inhale for five seconds, exhale for five seconds
3. Inhale for six seconds, exhale for six seconds (true resonance)
4. Inhale for five seconds, exhale for seven seconds

RECOMMENDATION

Utilize the night sky screen with tones for inhale and a lower tone for exhale, allowing closed eyes for a more immersive experience. This not only facilitates a deeper connection but also entrains brainwaves. The key to optimal results lies in consistent practice. Begin with one technique and observe its impact.

Shadow work is a significant commitment to the pursuit of self-discovery and personal development. To enhance the efficacy of this intricate process, it is imperative to integrate grounding techniques into one's practice, serving as a stabilizing force amid the often-tumultuous waves of emotions and memories that may surface.

One may engage in this preparatory ritual by closing their eyes, taking measured breaths, and actively sensing the connection between the body and the earth beneath. The tangible support of the ground during this moment serves as a reassuring acknowledgment of being firmly rooted in the present moment, preparing the individual for the forthcoming revelations (Kabat-Zinn, 2003).

ESTABLISHING A FOUNDATIONAL RITUAL: COMMENCING WITH GROUNDING

Viewed as an intimate dialogue with the inner self, each shadow work session benefits from a deliberate commencement with grounding techniques. This initial phase is likened to laying the cornerstone of a structure, providing a stable foundation upon which the entire exploration can rest. According to Dr. Jon Kabat-Zinn, a renowned expert in mindfulness, this deliberate grounding ritual is instrumental in fostering a heightened state of awareness, essential for effective self-exploration (Kabat-Zinn, 2003).

One may engage in this preparatory ritual by closing their eyes, taking measured breaths, and actively sensing the connection between the body and the earth beneath. The tangible support of the ground during this moment serves as a reassuring acknowledgment of being firmly rooted in the present moment, preparing the individual for the forthcoming revelations (Kabat-Zinn, 2003).

GROUNDING THROUGHOUT THE SESSION

As the exploration dives deep into the recesses of the subconscious, the likelihood of encountering intense emotions or memories is heightened. In such instances, grounding techniques function as a compass, aiding in navigation through potentially turbulent emotional waters. Grounding becomes a crucial tool, providing a lifeline when emotions surge, enabling individuals to maintain a state of presence throughout the process (Siegel, 2010).

Drawing inspiration from the work of Dr. Daniel J. Siegel, a leading expert in the field of interpersonal neurobiology, incorporating grounding techniques throughout the session ensures that individuals remain attuned to their emotions without becoming overwhelmed (Siegel, 2010). Whether through breath exercises, tactile awareness, or visualization techniques, grounding offers a structured approach to managing intense emotional experiences.

THE EVOLUTION OF GROUNDING: A NATURAL PROGRESSION

Integration of grounding techniques into the shadow work practice is a dynamic process that evolves with continued engagement. With each session, grounding transitions from a deliberate practice into an intuitive response, seamlessly woven into the fabric of the individual's self-discovery journey. This natural progression aligns with the principles of neuroplasticity, whereby repeated engagement with grounding techniques solidifies neural pathways associated with emotional regulation (Cozolino, 2014).

As comfort with grounding deepens, individuals discover increased resilience when confronting challenging aspects of their shadow work. Difficult memories and emotions cease to be formidable obstacles, transforming into constructive elements of the transformativeprocess. Trust in one's breath and senses, and visualization becomes second nature, contributing to a sense of security amid the exploration (Cozolino, 2014).

A GROUNDED AND EMPOWERED JOURNEY

In conclusion, the commitment to incorporating grounding techniques into the shadow work practice signifies a conscious effort to enhance the effectiveness of this transformative journey. Grounding, extending beyond a mere technique, emerges as a companion in the exploration of the self, offering support as individuals navigate the intricacies of their inner landscape.

This commitment is not without substantiated basis; experts such as Kabat-Zinn, Siegel, and Cozolino provide insights into the neurological and psychological underpinnings of grounding techniques. Grounding, when used intentionally and consistently, ensures that the shadow work journey is marked by resilience, empowerment, and a profound connection to the individual's unique essence.

There's something truly remarkable about the act of putting pen to paper or fingers to keys and just letting your thoughts flow onto the page. Have you ever tried journaling?

I stumbled upon the habit of journaling a while back, and it's become my go-to method for sorting through the chaos of everyday life. It's like having a private space where you can untangle your thoughts, reflect on your experiences, and even discover hidden gems within your own mind.

What I find fascinating is the way journaling gives you a tangible record of your personal growth. It's like flipping through the pages of your own story and seeing how far you've come. The power of putting your thoughts on paper is like capturing a moment in time, allowing you to revisit your past self and learn from the journey.

I've found that the simple act of journaling has not only improved my self-awareness but has also been a source of inspiration. It's amazing how ideas and solutions seem to materialize when you give your mind the freedom to wander on the pages of a journal.

Have you ever considered giving it a try? It might surprise you how liberating and empowering it can be. Turn to the next page to find out more!

CHAPTER 5:
THE POWER OF THE PEN:
JOURNALING
FOR SHADOW WORK

> *Writing in a daily journal is important but the reason why I journal is because I can read my own writing after many months have passed by. I'm able to reflect on my life, my actions, my behaviors, my memories and also the behavior of others around me.*
> *— Nando Prudhomme*

Do you ever think about how something incredibly powerful for personal growth may be right within your reach?

Surprisingly, it's not about hitting the gym hard or perfecting your sleep routine (although those are fantastic habits). It's actually something even simpler—the beautiful act of journaling.

Even though people have been doing it for centuries, journaling is getting a lot of attention these days. From self-help conversations to well-known figures like Deepak Chopra, everyone is buzzing about the life-changing benefits that come from making journaling a part of your routine.

Despite its recent popularity, this isn't just another trendy self-help thing. If you stick with it, journaling can truly make a difference in your mental strength, emotional well-being, and even your physical health.

Let's talk about why keeping a journal is so important and figure out some easy ways to weave this powerful habit into your everyday life.

WHAT IS JOURNALING?

Journaling is essentially the practice of putting your thoughts and feelings on paper as you navigate the ups and downs of daily life. It's a valuable tool that can aid in understanding and processing emotions, particularly during times of anxiety or sadness. Beyond that, journaling contributes to personal growth, self-awareness, and the discovery of meaningful insights.

The beauty of journaling lies in its adaptability; there's no fixed way to go about it. One day, it might resemble a traditional diary entry, reminiscent of those teenage years. The next day, it could transform into a list, highlighting things that bring you joy or outlining goals you aspire to achieve.

Cultivating a journaling habit is like having a reliable companion to help you navigate your emotions. It becomes a medium for personal growth, fostering self-awareness, and providing valuable insights. It's no wonder that many successful individuals, such as Richard Branson, Warren Buffet, and Arianna Huffington, have embraced journaling throughout their lives.

UNCOVERING YOUR HIDDEN SELF THROUGH JOURNALING

If you're keen on finding a way into your emotions and memories, using a journal could be an awesome way to go about it.

Whether you're just starting out with shadow work or have been at it for years, jotting down your thoughts and feelings can be a fantastic way to connect with your past and take steps toward moving forward.

This becomes particularly helpful when you're dealing with past traumas or experiences that have left emotional marks still impacting your present. Writing things down becomes like a therapeutic release, almost as if you're pulling out those toxic thoughts from your mind and putting them on paper.

And here's the cool part—keeping a journal can also help you spot patterns in your life. Maybe you've noticed that whenever you go on vacation, something not-so-great happens. Or perhaps, every time someone asks how you're doing, a bit of snarkiness comes out. Journaling gives us a chance to reflect on these patterns so we can start working with them in a way that sets us on the path to positive change in our lives.

WHAT IS A SHADOW WORK JOURNAL?

A shadow work journal is essentially a written companion designed to guide you through the process of reflecting on your shadow aspects and bringing them into the light. When we put our feelings into words on paper, it provides a powerful tool for understanding those parts of ourselves that we often try to overlook. This reflective practice gradually clears away negative patterns, preventing them from continuing to impact our lives adversely. Whether you choose to keep your journal digitally or opt for the traditional pen-and-paper approach, jotting down your thoughts, feelings, and emotions offers a transformative journey toward a deeper understanding of yourself.

WHY SHOULD WE USE A JOURNAL?

Why choose journaling, you ask? Well, let me tell you—it's like having a personal guide to explore those bits of ourselves we might usually shy away from. It nudges us to confront the uncomfortable or overlooked aspects, forcing us to face our shadow side and put into words what's often left unsaid.

And here's the beauty of it: journaling provides a structured way to work with your shadow, making it super accessible, especially if inner exploration is a new concept for you. Putting your thoughts on paper makes your challenges feel real and conquerable, sending a signal to your brain that change is possible.

But that's not all. Keeping a journal as you navigate your shadow work journey isn't just about today—it's about tracking your progress and finding those insightful connections later on. It's a chance to reflect on your life, see how things intertwine, and measure how far you've come. Journaling becomes a mirror reflecting your growth and a compass guiding you past the obstacles that once held you back.

STARTING A SHADOW WORK JOURNAL

There are a bunch of ways to kick it off, and it's totally up to you how you want to roll with it. Grab an old-school notebook and pen, or keep it tech-savvy with an app on your phone or tablet. There are cool digital journaling services like Day One or Evernote, too. The key is to find a place, whether it's physical or digital, where you can jot down your thoughts and untangle those shadowy corners.

Once your journal is in hand (or on your screen), don't overthink it—just open it up and start pouring out your thoughts. Seriously, you don't need to be some fancy writer. Just grab something to write with and let it flow. Maybe jot down what's buzzing in your mind, dig into a journal prompt, or unravel an event from your day—totally your call! It's your journal, your journey.

USING SHADOW WORK PROMPTS

Using shadow work prompts or questions is a bit like having a guide for your self-discovery journey. You can either pick from premade prompts or create your own, tailoring them to what feels right for you. At the end of this book is a selection of prompts for you to use.

Some prompts might take you deeper than others and they might stir up some discomfort—but that discomfort often signals something important for you to explore. It's like shining a light on the corners that need a little attention.

When you're faced with these prompts, give them the time they deserve. Write down anything that pops into your head. This isn't about judgment or shame; it's about making sense of those feelings, letting them unfold naturally instead of getting caught up in a never-ending loop of self-critique.

Now, here's the thing—after doing shadow work, taking care of yourself is key. It's important to give your mind a soothing balm. I'm all about meditation, taking a stroll, or whatever self-care act brings you joy. So, as you embark on this journey with your prompts, remember to be kind to yourself and maybe throw in some self-care magic afterward.

Below are some beginner friendly shadow work prompts:

1. How do you define self-love for yourself?

....

....

....

2. Recall a moment when you felt betrayed. What emotions arise?

....

....

....

3. Reflect on a time when you experienced rejection. How did it impact you?

....

....

....

4. Can you identify any repressed feelings within you? How do they manifest in your life?

....

....

....

5. List some qualities you believe are your strengths.

....

....

....

6. Acknowledge traits you consider less favorable about yourself.

....

....

....

7. Recollect a complex childhood memory. How does it still resonate with you?

....

....

....

8. Define personal development in your own terms.

....

....

....

9. In what areas could you reinforce boundaries more consistently?

....

....

....

10. Outline your core values. How do they guide your decisions?

....

....

....

11. Name a characteristic in others that you wish to embody.

....

....

....

12. Reflect on your childhood. What were you like as a child?

....

....

....

13. Craft a self-acceptance affirmation for yourself.

....
....
....

14. Identify something you fear doing. What holds you back?

....
....
....

15. Revisit the self-acceptance affirmation you wrote. How does it make you feel?

....
....
....

16. Understand your parents' values and how they shape your perspective.

....
....
....

17. Examine your stress-coping mechanisms. Are they healthy?

....
....
....

18. Explore what triggers jealousy in you and why.

....
....
....

19. Identify your triggers and the underlying reasons for them.

....

....

....

20. Describe a time when you engaged in self-sabotage. What motivated that behavior?

....

....

....

21. Reflect on your biggest regret and the lessons it holds.

....

....

....

22. Consider if you feel respected by those around you.

....

....

....

23. Evaluate your self-care practices. Can they be enhanced?

....

....

....

24. Explore if you ever deceive yourself to avoid confronting fears.

....

....

....

25. Identify emotions you tend to avoid. Why?

....
....
....

26. Reflect on your ability to forgive yourself after making mistakes.

....
....
....

27. Assess your contentment when alone.

....
....
....

28. Examine how you respond to constructive criticism.

....
....
....

29. Reflect on any sense of competition with someone in your life.

....
....
....

30. Explore if you feel misunderstood and in what ways.

....
....
....

31. Clarify your goals for the shadow work journey.

....

....

....

32. Compare and contrast yourself with your parents. How are you alike, and how are you different?

....

....

....

33. Describe your current life to your child self. What advice would you give?

....

....

....

34. Define what failure means to you and how it shapes your actions.

....

....

....

35. Identify behaviors in others that evoke strong reactions in you. Why do they upset you?

....

....

....

USING PREMADE JOURNAL PROMPTS FOR PERSONAL GROWTH

So, when it comes to these prompts, remember this: the good ones are the ones that make you squirm a bit. They might hit some nerves and stir things up, but that's exactly what makes them effective. They're like little keys unlocking the stuff that's holding you back, helping you heal and move forward.

Here's the trick! Sometimes, you might not even realize those beliefs are negative. So, approach the whole thing with an open mind, ready to shift your perspective if needed. It's like a journey of self-discovery, and you're the captain.

SHADOW WORK JOURNALING PROCESS

So, you might have heard that shadow work is often associated with working alongside a therapist, but here's the scoop—you can absolutely rock the solo journey! In fact, most of the time, you're fully equipped to tackle shadow work on your own. All it takes is an open mind and a willingness to shake up your world view. And trust me, when done right, it's not just about facing your demons; it's a game-changer that can make you more at ease in your own skin and ultimately boost your happiness.

Now, let me clarify—shadow work isn't reserved for those who've been through trauma. Rather, it's a fantastic tool for anyone eager to dive deep, understand themselves better, and amp up that self-awareness.

So, what's the deal with shadow work? It's all about confronting those parts of yourself you've been brushing aside or hiding. It's about digging into your own pain and shame, bringing it into the light, and examining it from every angle until it starts making sense.

You can break down the process into four key steps:

STEP 1: RECOGNIZE

Uncovering your shadow aspects can be a challenging journey. However, it's crucial to acknowledge that these aspects exist within you, shaping and influencing you in various ways.

To overcome the initial apprehension of identifying these aspects, start by taking stock of your current emotional state. What feelings are present at this moment? What thoughts are circulating in your mind? What beliefs do you hold about yourself?

Following this, make an effort to articulate your emotions, beliefs, and thoughts. This encompasses a range of feelings like guilt, shame, inadequacy, anger, resentment, sadness, and even fear of abandonment—whatever resonates with you. Once you've compiled and named this list, you'll gain a clearer understanding of how each aspect impacts your daily life and why certain experiences may be unfolding in your present.

STEP 2: EMBRACE AND EMBRACE MORE

Now, let's look at how to understand those shadow aspects—it's all about welcoming your emotions, and that includes the ones that might not be your favorites. Be kind to yourself in this process. How you navigate negative emotions often stems from past experiences, so cut yourself some slack! Compassion is key, but it's equally crucial not to let it hinder your honesty about what you're going through.

When we talk about emotions, it's common to label them as either good or bad—but truth be told, emotions are just energy, each holding its unique value. If we can grasp that every emotion has its place, we start seeing even the aspects we don't fancy about ourselves as potentially useful.

Accept their existence, acknowledge that they're part of you.

In the realm of shadow work, you gaze at these less-than-ideal traits as integral to your identity—not as something to be ashamed of or concealed. It's about understanding how they interplay with your overall personality and impact your life. Armed with this knowledge, you can craft a more balanced and joyful life.

Take anger, for instance. Instead of trying to stifle or hide it, you might discover that anger serves as a vehicle for expressing your stance against injustice or unfairness. This realization allows you to embrace anger as just another facet of who you are—no need to "fix" it, but rather to understand and integrate it.

STEP 3: GRASP THE WHY

So, you've acknowledged those aspects; now, let's understand them on a deeper level. Once you've acknowledged that a specific facet exists within you and doesn't need to be tamed or erased, ask yourself: How does it serve you right now? For instance, "Does my anger empower me?" or "Is fear a tool for keeping me safe?"

These emotions might be stirred up by a trigger—maybe a work issue or just a challenging day. But getting to the root of your emotions matters. It aids in processing and integrating them into your being without carrying the weight of shame or guilt.

Understanding the why behind your emotions can take various routes: you might question, "What does this feeling make me desire?" or seek external resources to shed light on your emotions. Another avenue is turning to someone close for advice on how they would navigate your situation.

Sometimes, your emotional response could be linked to your beliefs, or it might be triggered by an event echoing the past. Go ahead, delve into the WHY of your feelings. It's all part of the journey toward self-discovery and growth.

STEP 4: INTEGRATE

As we look into the mirror of our own being, those shadow aspects can feel like a tidal wave of overwhelming complexities. We spot parts of ourselves that we wish were different, and the instinct to shield those parts from the world may kick in. But here's the twist: when we engage in this internal battle, we're essentially fighting against ourselves, and that friction spills over into our lives, causing disruptions.

Now, envision this: when we perceive our shadow aspects not as problems but as integral parts of ourselves, the script of life can flip for the better. Instead of resisting, we can start collaborating with these aspects. Here's how you can dive into this process:

Ask yourself questions like:
- What does this aspect need?
- How can I support it?
- In what way does it want to be seen?
- What aspirations does it harbor for my life?

Discovering how to collaborate with your shadow aspects, rather than working in opposition, is a pivotal step toward a happier and more fulfilling life! It's a journey of integration, a dance with the different facets of yourself, leading to a harmonious and thriving existence.

HOW CAN YOU EFFECTIVELY NAVIGATE YOUR SHADOW WORK JOURNAL WITH A STRAIGHTFORWARD PROCESS?

LET'S START WITH STEP 1: CRAFT A GAME PLAN

Take a moment to figure out how often you'd like to delve into your shadow aspects. While it's often recommended to do this daily or every other day for optimal results, if you're just starting, consider allowing more time between sessions to digest and fully absorb what you uncover. Find a schedule that feels right for you in the present moment.

Now, decide when you want to embark on your prompts ritual—whether it's in the morning, evening, or any other part of the day. Choose a time when you can be fully present and free from interruptions. Also, pinpoint what specific area you want to focus on—perhaps there's a particular challenge or issue you're eager to address. It's your journey, so tailor it to suit your needs.

NOW ONTO STEP 2: SET UP YOUR SANCTUARY

To truly concentrate, we require a secure space where interruptions are out of the question. It's about creating both a physical haven and dedicating ample time to sift through our thoughts without the looming specter of judgment or fear of interference from others.

STEP 3: EASE INTO IT

Hold off on the writing for a moment. Allow yourself the time to gather your thoughts and center yourself—the aim is to be fully present in the moment, not mentally elsewhere. Taking a brief moment to relax not only helps ground you but also cultivates a sense of safety, especially when delving into potentially uncomfortable topics. Whether it's a short meditation or listening to your favorite music, do whatever brings you a sense of calm and readiness.

STEP 4: CONCENTRATE AND REFLECT

This step is straightforward. Engage with your chosen journal prompt or contemplate the issue you wish to explore. When you sense readiness, begin putting your thoughts into words. It's your time to focus and let the words flow.

STEP 5: ACCEPT WHATEVER ARISES

Give your mind the freedom to unveil memories, thoughts, and feelings without passing them through the filters of "good/bad" or "relevant/stupid." Make a pact with yourself for the next 10–15 minutes: whatever surfaces, you'll jot it down. No judgment, no criticism.

It's completely normal to feel a bit uneasy or uncomfortable with certain thoughts—that's the essence of shadow work. Be open to surprises; you might just uncover something unexpected.

STEP 6: UNCOVER YOUR TRIGGERS AND PATTERNS

Once your thoughts are on paper, take a moment for thoughtful analysis. You might notice recurring patterns—perhaps you respond similarly to certain triggers or consistently draw in individuals with specific characteristics.

Once these patterns reveal themselves, delve into the why. Explore their origins and causes. Yes, it involves more writing on your part.

Be keenly aware of how these patterns and triggers shape your decisions, responses, and, ultimately, the overall quality of your life. It's about gaining insight into the forces that guide your actions.

STEP 7: TAKE YOUR INSIGHTS ALONG

It might sound a bit ominous, but it's quite straightforward. Don't confine your work to the journal. When you put it away, let it stay with you in spirit. The next time you're out and about, turn your attention inward. Observe those triggers and patterns, notice how they weave into your daily life, and make a conscious effort to be mindful of your reactions and emotions. Let your newfound understanding be a companion in your day-to-day experiences.

Keep this in mind…

Approach this journey with an open mind. Shadow work is a transformative process that allows you to cleanse your subconscious, paving the way for a life of freedom, peace, and acceptance. It's no walk in the park, but the rewards are truly worthwhile.

CONSIDER THESE THREE MINDSET TIPS

1. Accept authenticity and honesty, even when it feels uncomfortable. Looking into the depths of your psyche to unearth the truth about who you are can be intimidating. However, the more genuine and truthful you are with yourself, the greater the long-term benefits.

2. Grant yourself the freedom to explore your psyche without judgment. Shadow work involves confronting aspects of yourself that may not be aesthetically pleasing, such as fears and insecurities. Yet, don't let that deter you. Remember that everyone has shadows—they're an integral part of our shared human experience. As long as the exploration is respectful, there's nothing wrong with delving into these aspects openly and honestly.

3. Fearlessly challenge your beliefs and opinions, no matter how deeply ingrained they may be. Understand that, while our thoughts may seem like absolute truths in the moment, they aren't necessarily enduring truths. So, don't shy away from stepping outside your comfort zone. Your growth lies in the willingness to question and evolve.

Approach your shadow work with care, especially if you're going at it on your own.

Remember...

Looking into your shadow is a tough yet crucial process for personal growth and healing. It demands courage and strength, but it can turn risky if not approached correctly.

As you step into shadow work, ensure you take it slow. Resist the temptation to hurriedly explore emotionally challenging areas, as it could potentially worsen things.

Allow intervals between your shadow work sessions for thoughtful reflection and to ensure a smooth emotional flow before moving on to the next phase.

It's quite common to become absorbed in the exploration of your shadow, but always keep in mind that you're a person with emotions and needs. Excessive pushing may do more harm than good.

Shadow work isn't a quick fix; it's a gradual journey requiring time and patience. Prioritize self-care and remember, the people around you are there to offer support. You're not navigating this journey alone.

Discover your own approach!

Engaging in shadow work doesn't have to be a daily grind (although you totally can if you want to). There are various ways to dive into shadow work and journaling, and the magic lies in finding what suits you best.

Some folks like writing down their thoughts in a journal or notebook. Others prefer expressing their emotions through drawings or artistic creations. And then there are those who weave their feelings into music or other forms of art. It's like a choose-your-own-adventure, but for introspection!

You might discover that one method clicks more than the others, but the key is to stay open-minded and notice what brings you the results you're looking for—whatever they may be!

Shadow work is like the hero's journey in your personal healing saga. It lets you confront your inner demons and make peace with them. It's not a task to rush or procrastinate because, let's face it, "later" might never come if we don't start now. Think of shadow work as a lifelong buddy, evolving as you evolve as an individual and as a human being.

We all have our quirky methods for facing our shadows, whether it's pouring thoughts into a journal or having a heart-to-heart with someone who gets it. No strict rules apply to this work; all you need is an open mind and the willingness to experiment until you find what clicks for you! Yes, it's a bit challenging and weighty, but the payoff is incredibly gratifying.

Now have you ever wondered if there's a secret technique for shadow work that doesn't involve journaling? What if there's a captivating method waiting to be uncovered—one that sparks creativity and deep self-discovery? Intrigued? Turn to the next page and plunge into the world of unconventional techniques that might just revolutionize your journey of introspection!

CHAPTER 6:
FINDING CALM IN CHAOS:
MINDFULNESS AND MEDITATION
IN SHADOW WORK

In this chapter, I want to share with you some mindfulness and meditation techniques that have the potential to elevate your experience with shadow work. While I want to emphasize that meditation isn't a must for shadow work, think of it as a helpful tool that can anchor you and draw you nearer to your inner thoughts. Let's explore these practices together and see how they might enhance our journey of self-discovery.

WHAT IS MEDITATION?

Have you ever wondered about the art of meditation? It's a beautiful practice that involves channeling your focus and clearing your mind through a blend of mental and physical techniques.

Choosing the right meditation style allows you to experience a range of benefits, from relaxation and stress reduction to improved mental well-being. Some even turn to meditation as a tool for enhancing their overall health, using it as support in overcoming challenges such as quitting tobacco.

Although meditation has roots that span thousands of years and various cultural traditions, it's only in recent decades that modern science has delved deeply into its study. Thanks to cutting-edge technology, such as electroencephalography (EEG) and functional magnetic resonance imaging (fMRI) scans, we've made significant strides in understanding the profound impact of meditation on the brain.

When you observe someone meditating, it may appear as simple as rhythmic breathing or the repetition of a soothing phrase. However, within their mind, a remarkable transformation is occurring. Modern diagnostic tools reveal that meditation can have a positive influence on both the brain and mental health. So, if you're considering taking this journey, know that it's not just a practice—it's a path to inner well-being and discovery.

Meditation finds its roots in ancient philosophies and various world religions, but the beauty of it lies in its inclusivity—you don't need to adhere to a particular religion to embrace meditation.

Let's dig into the rich fabric of both religious and nonreligious meditation methods:

Buddhist: Originating in Buddhism, which is both a philosophy and religion, meditation takes diverse forms. Theravadin meditation is prevalent in Southeast Asia, particularly in India and Thailand, while Zen Buddhist meditation has its roots in China, evolving into different forms such as Japanese Zen Buddhist meditation. Tibetan Buddhist tantric meditation originated in Tibet, now an autonomous region of China.

Christian: Contemplation, a practice where intense focus is directed toward questions, ideas, religious concepts, or deities, is common in Christianity. Prayer, especially in contemplative forms, is often recognized as a meditative practice.

Guided: This nonreligious meditation form can be group-based or one-on-one, commonly used in counseling, therapy, and support settings.

Osho: Also known as "dynamic meditation," this form has Hindu roots from India. It involves deliberate and forceful breathing exercises.

Sufi: Found within the branch of Islam known as Sufism, meditation is a prevalent practice among its followers.

Taoist: Similar to Buddhism, Taoism is both a religion and philosophy originating in China, notably through the teachings of Laozi.

Transcendental: Hailing from India, this nonreligious meditation involves the repetition of mantras, phrases or words that individuals focus on either aloud or in their minds.

Yoga: Originating in India, yoga represents both a physical and meditative practice, existing in both religious and nonreligious forms.

In essence, meditation is a versatile journey that welcomes practitioners from various walks of life, making it accessible and beneficial regardless of religious affiliation.

Meditation holds the key to enhancing your quality of life, unlocking a myriad of psychological and physical advantages validated by scientific research. Here are 10 evidence-backed benefits of meditation:

1. STRESS REDUCTION

Scientific studies highlight that mindfulness-based interventions like meditation effectively alleviate stress. By regulating cortisol levels, the hormone responsible for the body's stress response, meditation becomes a powerful tool in mitigating chronic stress and its adverse effects on cardiovascular health, the immune system, and gut health.

2. ANXIETY MANAGEMENT

Meditation acts as a calming force against anxiety, slowing down racing thoughts and regulating breathing to soothe the nervous system. Long-term meditation practice demonstrates positive impacts on mental health, reducing overwhelming feelings of fear, worry, and tension.

3. DEPRESSION MANAGEMENT

Through the lenses of mindfulness and emotional regulation, meditation contributes to reducing depression symptoms. Participants in a 3-month yoga and meditation retreat displayed significant improvements in depression, stress resilience, and overall well-being, as observed in a study.

4. LOWERS BLOOD PRESSURE

Meditation, when coupled with a healthy lifestyle, shows promise in lowering high blood pressure, a prevalent condition affecting millions worldwide. While more research is needed to understand specific impacts across meditation types, existing evidence suggests a potential benefit.

5. STRENGTHENS IMMUNE SYSTEM HEALTH

Consistent meditation emerges as an effective behavioral treatment for conditions linked to a weakened immune system. By reducing the body's stress response, meditation lowers inflammation and decreases the risk of chronic pain, fatigue, and heart disease.

6. IMPROVES MEMORY

Beyond stress relief, meditation positively influences brain structure by increasing gray matter production, essential for healthy cognition and the protection of memory-related areas. Thirty minutes of daily meditation over 8 weeks has been associated with a significant increase in gray matter production.

7. REGULATES MOOD

Regular meditation transforms emotional reactions by fostering mindfulness and controlled breathing. This, over time, leads to less impulsive responses, enabling individuals to regulate their mood effectively even in challenging situations.

8. INCREASES SELF-AWARENESS

Meditation nurtures self-awareness by fostering a habit of focusing on the present moment. Research indicates that practicing meditation enhances self-awareness, impulse control, and interpersonal relationships.

9. HELPS WITH ADDICTION MANAGEMENT

The calming and stress-reducing effects of meditation play a pivotal role in aiding individuals with substance use disorders. It promotes abstinence maintenance, helps manage triggers, and diminishes cravings associated with anxiety or stress.

10. IMPROVES SLEEP

Research suggests that meditation can enhance sleep quality and address issues like insomnia and daytime sleep-related problems. While further exploration is needed, meditation has shown promising effects in alleviating the mental rumination that often interferes with restful sleep.

Incorporating meditation into your daily routine holds the potential to not only transform your mental landscape but also fortify your physical well-being based on a foundation of scientific validation.

Research consistently supports the benefits of meditation for mental well-being and cognitive function. A published study by Tang et al. (2007) found that regular meditation can lead to structural changes in the brain, specifically in areas associated with attention and sensory processing.

Furthermore, a meta-analysis conducted by Goyal et al. (2014), which reviewed 47 trials involving over 3,500 participants, concluded that mindfulness meditation programs show moderate evidence of improving anxiety, depression, and pain. This adds robust support to the idea that meditation is not merely a subjective experience but has measurable positive effects on mental health.

In the context of meditation for beginners, research by Zeidan et al. (2010) demonstrated that even short-term meditation training can result in improved cognitive control. This counters the misconception that meditation is only effective after years of practice and highlights its potential for immediate cognitive benefits.

Regarding the use of meditation in shadow work, there is growing interest in the psychological community. A study by Ho (2014) explored the integration of mindfulness meditation into psychotherapy, emphasizing its potential for enhancing self-awareness and emotional regulation. This aligns with the idea that meditation creates a space for non-judgmental self-reflection, crucial in shadow work.

Moreover, a systematic review by Khoury et al. (2013) found that mindfulness meditation interventions are effective in reducing symptoms of anxiety and depression. This suggests that the calming effects of meditation can be particularly valuable in creating a conducive environment for individuals engaged in the often emotionally intense process of shadow work.

Practical applications of meditation in psychological interventions are gaining recognition. A randomized controlled trial by Hölzel et al. (2011) observed structural brain changes in areas associated with self-awareness and compassion after an 8-week mindfulness-based stress reduction (MBSR) program. This reinforces the idea that meditation not only impacts subjective experience but also induces measurable changes in brain structure.

The practice of meditation, when understood beyond common misconceptions, emerges as a scientifically-supported method for enhancing mental well-being, cognitive function, and self-awareness. The integration of meditation into shadow work aligns with this, providing a structured approach to self-exploration and healing, supported by both experiential accounts and empirical research.

HOW TO MEDITATE FOR HEALING

People turn to meditation with diverse aims—be it for the physical, mental, or relational benefits it offers. Some are drawn to meditation for personal growth, emotional healing, or spiritual development. Regardless of the initial motivation, probing into meditation over time unveils aspects of oneself, some of which may be less than comfortable—a world often referred to as the "shadow self."

Our personality, shaped by conscious thoughts, emotions, decisions, and interactions, plays out on the surface of our conscious mind. However, this is just the visible part of the iceberg. Eastern contemplative philosophies and modern Western psychology alike propose that beneath this conscious layer lies the subconscious and, even deeper, the unconscious mind.

The content dwelling in our subconscious and unconscious minds structures our personality. These hidden forces shape our decisions, thoughts, and feelings. Despite their profound influence, we know little about them as our conscious mind remains occupied and frenetic, rarely providing the opportunity to explore these deeper layers.

Isn't it unsettling to consider that the aspects that wield the most influence on your life are often the ones you're least conscious of?

Meditation unfolds as a powerful ally in this regard by quieting the conscious mind, providing a space to connect with the depths beneath the surface. Simultaneously, this presents one of meditation's significant challenges—a hurdle that many might not anticipate or recognize.

As meditation progresses, our focus begins to plunge into the subconscious. The conscious mind, now less preoccupied, allows awareness to retreat to deeper layers of our being. In this space, elements that were once repressed or consciously overlooked in life come to the forefront.

These may encompass:

- *Difficult emotions*
- *Hidden traumas*
- *Wild desires*
- *Complexes*
- *Negative thought patterns*
- *Feelings of shame, guilt, and regret*
- *Aggressiveness and anger*
- *Unconscious fears*
- *Unresolved emotional processes*

Encountering this array for the first time can be unsettling for a novice meditator. Thoughts like, "Since I started meditating, my mind feels busier," or "Meditation is making me more anxious and restless," may arise.

The truth is, meditation isn't causing your mind to become noisier or more anxious; rather, it unveils the preexisting noise and anxiety. With fewer distractions, these aspects become unmistakably clear. It's akin to letting a cup of muddy water settle, revealing all the dirt that was already present.

In addition to fostering calm and clarity, meditation heightens sensitivity and sharpens attention, enabling you to perceive aspects of yourself that were previously hidden. Energies trapped in your psyche begin to surface. It's like opening the "Pandora's box" of your subconscious mind—a process that may not always be pleasant but signifies progress in your meditation practice.

In essence, you are encountering and liberating your shadow self!

Before you begin any shadow work, it's key to set up a comfy and safe spot where you can really get into the process. Find a quiet nook, away from any disruptions. Some folks like to add a touch of Zen by lighting up candles, burning incense, or playing some chill tunes.

Don't forget to tidy up your space—clean and organized. A neat spot helps clear your mind, making your meditation time more focused and productive.

SETTING YOUR FOCUS

Before you kick off your shadow work meditation, take a beat to set some intentions. It's like giving your mind a roadmap for the session. Your intention could be super specific, like letting go of a certain feeling or tackling a particular issue. Or, it could just be a general vibe of being open to whatever comes up during the meditation.

Consider writing down your intention and keeping it close by during the meditation – a little reminder of why you're on this journey in the first place.

GROUND YOURSELF

Once you've found a comfortable space to sit, ensure your back is straight and your feet are firmly planted on the ground. Close your eyes and take a few deep cycles of breath through the nose, allowing the breath to center you and create a sense of inner calm. Feel the connection between your body and the earth beneath you.

ACCEPTANCE

Embrace a genuine and nonjudgmental attitude toward yourself. Allow honesty to flow as you acknowledge and accept the various aspects of your being. This step involves opening up to the reality of your thoughts, feelings, and experiences without self-criticism.

OBSERVE

Shift your awareness inward and delve into the exploration of your shadow self. Option A involves imagining a shadow trait that you are aware of but may have been avoiding. Option B encourages visualizing a past event that holds emotional significance, seeking clarity about how it has shaped your shadow self. This introspective exercise helps illuminate hidden aspects of your psyche.

MEET YOUR SHADOW

As you engage with your shadow self, be present with the emotions that arise. Allow the shadow to communicate with you, either through thoughts, sensations, or images. Listen attentively to what your shadow has to tell you, understanding that these aspects are a natural part of your humanity.

PRACTICE GRATITUDE

Express gratitude toward the emotions and insights that surface during this exploration. Acknowledge that your shadow self, though sometimes challenging, plays a crucial role in your personal growth and self-awareness. Gratitude can foster a positive relationship with these aspects of yourself.

INTEGRATION

Embrace the discovered emotions and insights as integral parts of your identity. Recognize that your shadow self is not something to be rejected or suppressed, but rather an essential aspect of your whole being. This step involves accepting and integrating these aspects, fostering a holistic and balanced sense of self.

Keep in mind that your emotional journey can vary from session to session, and certain feelings may require revisiting before they become fully integrated. Be kind to yourself and give the process the time it deserves to blend these emotions into your being, including your shadow.

VISUALIZATION AND GUIDED IMAGERY

Using your imagination and guided imagery can be a powerful way to dive into your subconscious and connect with your shadow self. Here's a simple script to guide you through the process:

Imagine you're taking a stroll in a sunny forest. Birds are doing their thing, making a sweet melody.

While walking, you spot a cave. It calls to you, so you decide to check it out.

Inside, there's a soft light guiding you to a room.

In that room, there's a mirror. Look into it and notice any not-so-great parts of yourself that you might have been dodging.

Now, take a nice, deep breath. Accept those parts. See them becoming a natural part of who you are.

When you're ready, slowly come back to the now, open your eyes, and carry that wisdom with you.

POST-SHADOW WORK CARE AND INTEGRATION

After you've wrapped up your shadow work meditation, it's time to treat yourself with care. Exploring your shadow can stir up intense emotions, so consider indulging in self-care practices. A soothing bath, a nature walk, some heartfelt journaling, or quality time with loved ones can work wonders.

Integration is key in shadow work. Take the insights from your meditation and weave them into your daily existence. Reflect on what you've learned and how it connects to your life. Set intentions for changes based on these new insights. Throughout this process, be patient and gentle with yourself.

Now comes the action part. Post-shadow work, it's crucial to make tangible changes. This might mean setting boundaries, tweaking habits, or even seeking therapy. Remember that small steps are mighty, and consistency is key. Keep in mind, shadow work is a journey, so be patient and stay committed to creating lasting transformations.

Even if it feels strange at first, stick with it. Be patient. Your inner voice will speak up, either right then or later in the day. Doing nothing has this cool after-effect, like taking a time-release capsule of peace and wisdom. You'll experience synchronicities, get the advice you need, and have those "aha" moments. Plus, you'll realize you're way more than the discomfort or pain you might be feeling. Keep going—it's totally worth it.

Discovering a connection with my soul has been a game-changer for both my body and mind. It's like stumbling upon my true home. Once I found it, everything seemed to fall into place, and my body began its healing journey.

BALANCING MINDFULNESS AND MEDITATION IN SHADOW WORK

Let's now talk about finding your sweet spot between mindfulness and meditation as you navigate the intricate terrain of shadow work. Your journey is entirely your own, and there's no right or wrong way to do this. Let's break it down in a way that's easy to understand.

MINDFULNESS OR MEDITATION? PICK YOUR FLOW

So, when you are finally ready to get into shadow work, you've got these two buddies—mindfulness and meditation. Now, if you're the kind of person always buzzing with energy and can't sit still for too long, mindfulness might be your thing. It's all about bringing awareness to your everyday hustle, making your daily routine a canvas for self-reflection. Eating your cereal or strolling to the store suddenly becomes moments of Zen.

On the flip side, if you crave a bit more structure and focus, choose meditation. It's like a deep-dive session for your mind, offering a quiet space to explore your shadows with laser-like attention. It's your dedicated "me time" for some quality introspection.

Remember that it's not about fitting into someone else's mold. Your practice should groove with your vibe, not disrupt it.

MINDFULNESS AND MEDITATION ARE MORE THAN JUST TOOLS

Now, let's think beyond techniques—mindfulness and meditation are like sidekicks for life. Imagine sprinkling a bit of mindfulness and meditation into your everyday routine. It's not about finding time; it's about making these practices part of your day.

Maybe you've got a set time for meditation, creating a personal retreat where you can dig deep. Or perhaps, you're into infusing mindfulness into your daily grind, turning your usual chores into a self-discovery mission. Either way, it's about weaving these practices into the fabric of your life.

TAKE IT EASY: YOU'RE RIDING YOUR OWN WAVE

This journey isn't all rainbows and butterflies. It's normal to face bumps and discomfort. But guess what? You're not alone in this. Like Jon Kabat-Zinn once said, "You can't stop the waves, but you can learn to surf."

So, when those waves of thoughts and emotions crash in, ride them. Accept the chaos, and remember that you're getting better at this with every try. Be patient with yourself, because Rome wasn't built in a day.

SOME RECOMMENDATION FROM MY SIDE TO HELP YOU CULTIVATE INNER PEACE

Are you ready to rock the world of mindfulness and meditation? Here are some fantastic apps that can guide you on your journey to inner peace:

1. HEADSPACE: YOUR PERSONAL MINDFULNESS COACH

Headspace is like a personal guide in your pocket. It offers guided meditations, mindfulness exercises, and even sleep aids. The animations make it super user-friendly, perfect for beginners!

2. CALM: FIND YOUR CALM

Calm lives up to its name by providing a variety of guided meditations, soothing music, and sleep stories. It's like a spa for your mind, helping you find your inner calm amidst the chaos.

3. INSIGHT TIMER: CONNECT WITH A GLOBAL MEDITATION COMMUNITY

This app not only offers a vast library of guided meditations but also connects you with a global community of meditators. You can even see how many people around the world are meditating with you in real-time.

4. BREATHE: MINDFULNESS AND MEDITATION

Breathe is a fantastic app for quick, effective meditation sessions. It's perfect for busy bees, offering short exercises that you can seamlessly integrate into your daily routine.

5. SIMPLE HABIT: MEDITATION FOR BUSY PEOPLE

Simple Habit is designed with busy schedules in mind. With meditations ranging from five minutes to longer sessions, it's perfect for anyone looking to squeeze in a moment of mindfulness during a hectic day.

Remember that the key is consistency. Start with just a few minutes a day, and gradually increase as you feel more comfortable.

CHAPTER 7:
CONFRONTING THE PAST WITHOUT FEAR

> *Each of us must confront our own fears, and must come face to face with them. How we handle our fears will determine where we go with the rest of our lives. To experience adventure or to be limited by the fear of it.*
> — Judy Blume

In this chapter, I aim to empower you with practical strategies and exercises that will assist you in safely facing your past traumas and negative experiences. My goal is to break down the process into manageable steps, provide you with tools for emotional regulation, and offer reassurance at every stage of your journey.

It can be really tough to move on from the past. We all handle life experiences differently, and for some, letting go seems like an uphill battle. You know, some people breeze through tough times, while others feel the weight of those experiences lingering in their minds.

For those finding it hard to release certain events from their past, it might be because of some deep-seated trauma. Trauma is like this emotional wound that sticks around after something really distressing, be it loss, danger, or embarrassment. And it's not just tied to big, violent events like war; it can hit anyone and reshape how they see things.

Some people get caught up in rumination, where they can't stop thinking about the same stuff. It turns out that people who've been through tough times might believe that overthinking gives them insights. However, all that dwelling on the past can actually make it harder for them to move forward. It's a common thread in things such as depression, obsessive-compulsive disorder, anxiety, and PTSD.

But there are other reasons people hang on to the past. Sometimes, it's about holding onto the good stuff that's now just a memory. Or it might be a way to unconsciously shield themselves from getting hurt in the future. It's complex. Understanding and being there for someone dealing with this stuff can make a world of difference.

HOW TO DEAL WITH TRAUMA: FIVE SIMPLE APPROACHES

Regardless of the challenges you're facing, it's crucial to approach the healing process with compassion. While your experiences may remain a part of you, adopting constructive strategies can empower you to cope with symptoms and reconstruct your life.

According to Elizabeth Keohan, a therapist at Talkspace, "Embracing the journey of healing from trauma not only equips you with valuable tools but also enables a deeper understanding of triggers, defenses, and potential disruptions to your daily life. This process helps you navigate each day with reduced dysregulation and intensity, fostering a fuller engagement with the present rather than being tethered to the past, which may be hindering your progress."

STEP 1: RECOGNIZE YOUR EMOTIONS

Acknowledging your feelings is a crucial step in dealing with unresolved trauma. It might not be easy, but it's important to accept the emotions you're grappling with. Whether it's anger, guilt, or shock from what you've been through, let yourself feel these emotions without judgment. Trying to push them away or pretend they don't exist could lead to more stress in the long run.

Healing takes time, and it's okay if you're facing intense or unpredictable emotions. Remember that recovery doesn't happen overnight. Don't pressure yourself to return to normal quickly. Instead, be patient and give yourself the time needed to heal. If you feel overwhelmed, it's perfectly okay to recognize the signs that you might need a mental health day for yourself. Listen to what your mind and body are telling you.

STEP 2: PRIORITIZE SELF-CARE

When dealing with trauma, it's common to overlook your basic needs. Neglecting things like a healthy diet or sufficient sleep can worsen symptoms of traumatic stress. Taking better care of yourself is crucial for building the strength needed for recovery. Prioritizing self-care is essential for maintaining a balanced and healthy mind–body life.

For instance, many people face sleep troubles after a traumatic experience, but practicing good sleep hygiene can make it easier to get the rest you need. There's a strong connection between sleep and mental health. Additionally, incorporating exercise into your routine can improve your mood and aid in relaxation after a challenging day. The key takeaway is, when figuring out how to cope with trauma, don't forget to pay attention to your own health. Taking care of yourself lays the foundation for a more resilient recovery.

STEP 3: STAY CONNECTED WITH LOVED ONES

After a traumatic experience, it's natural to want to withdraw, but your relationships with family and friends can be a powerful source of strength. Research suggests that social support can even reduce the body's production of cortisol, a stress hormone, during anxious or overwhelming times.

You don't have to dive into discussing your trauma if you're not ready, but any form of social interaction can be beneficial. Simply spending time with people who you care about can contribute to a sense of normalcy and help you start feeling more like yourself again. Whether it's opening up about your experiences or enjoying simple, pleasant moments together, connecting with loved ones plays a vital role in the healing process.

STEP 4: REDUCE STRESS IN YOUR LIFE

While stress is something everyone faces, managing it can be particularly challenging during the recovery from trauma. It's important to work on minimizing stress in your life and finding healthy ways to cope with the stress you do experience.

Consider incorporating relaxation techniques into your routine to calm down when feeling overwhelmed. This can include:

- *Breathing exercises for anxiety*
- *Meditation for stress relief*
- *Yoga for relaxation*
- *Journaling for mental health*

Healing yourself is a courageous and empowering step. While the path might be challenging, remember that every small effort contributes to your well-being. In addition to the invaluable support of a trained therapist, there are activities you can explore in the comfort of your home. These activities, when coupled with professional guidance, can become powerful tools in your healing toolbox. So, let's look through a range of activities that promote self-discovery, mindfulness, and resilience. Remember that progress is a personal journey, and each step you take is a victory on the road to healing.

Here are some activities you can try at home to help with trauma:

GROUNDING EXERCISES
Bring yourself back to the present moment by deep breathing or focusing on your surroundings.

PROGRESSIVE MUSCLE RELAXATION
Tense and relax different muscle groups to promote relaxation and reduce physical tension.

SELF-COMPASSION EXERCISES
Cultivate kindness toward yourself through activities like writing a compassionate letter or practicing self-care.

JOURNALING
Write about your thoughts and feelings related to trauma, helping to process and understand your experiences.

MINDFULNESS MEDITATION
Focus on your breath or body sensations in the present moment, with guided meditations available online.

GRATITUDE PRACTICE
Reflect on things you are grateful for each day to foster appreciation and contentment.

BODY SCAN

Pay attention to each part of your body to increase awareness of physical sensations and tension.

MINDFUL BREATHING

Focus on your breath to become more present and grounded.

WALKING MEDITATION

Concentrate on the sensation of walking to promote mindfulness.

MINDFUL EATING

Eat slowly, savoring the taste, texture, and smell of food.

PAY ATTENTION

Use all five senses to notice your environment amid a busy world.

BE PRESENT

Bring open, accepting attention to everything you do, finding joy in simple pleasures.

FREE DRAWING AND PAINTING

Express yourself without a specific goal in mind.

COLLAGE-MAKING

Create collages using various materials to explore and express emotions.

CLAY SCULPTING

Make three-dimensional clay sculptures to process feelings in a tactile way.

MANDALA COLORING

Color predrawn mandalas for relaxation and creative expression.

MASK-MAKING

Create masks to explore and express different aspects of your personality or emotions.

LETTER WRITING

Express thoughts and feelings in a letter to yourself or others for emotional processing.

CREATIVE WRITING

Use short stories, poems, or other forms of writing to explore imagination and express emotions.

YOGA

Practice physical postures, breathing techniques, and meditation for relaxation and emotional balance.

TAI CHI

Engage in slow, gentle movements, deep breathing, and meditation for relaxation and well-being.

BREATHWORK

Use various breathing techniques to reduce stress and increase focus.

GUIDED IMAGERY

Visualize calming scenes or scenarios for relaxation and emotional well-being.

SELF-MASSAGE

Apply gentle pressure to soothe different parts of the body.

TAKING A BATH OR SHOWER

A calming experience to relax and refresh, enhanced with aromatherapy.

RELAXING HOBBIES

Engage in soothing hobbies like painting, drawing, knitting, or gardening.

POSITIVE SELF-TALK

Repeat affirmations to boost confidence and self-assurance.

PHYSICAL EXERCISE

Release endorphins through activities like walking or stretching for stress reduction and relaxation.

UNDERSTANDING YOUR EMOTIONS DURING DIFFICULT TIMES

In times of adversity, it's common for individuals to grapple with a spectrum of challenging emotions such as anger, confusion, fear, loneliness, and sadness. These emotions can be overpowering and have a significant impact on one's emotional well-being. Yet, the pathway to overcoming these difficulties often lies in the practice of mindfulness.

Mindfulness provides a space for individuals to calm themselves, fostering reflection and deliberate responses instead of reactive behaviors. The initial step in addressing challenging emotions is to embrace them with acceptance. This involves acknowledging the emotion and pinpointing where it manifests in the body, whether it's a stomachache, a tightened throat, a racing heart, or tension elsewhere. Rather than resisting the emotion, it's essential to sit with it and comprehend the message it is conveying.

Another crucial step in managing challenging emotions is to identify and label them. Instead of saying, "I am angry," try expressing, "This is anger" or "This is anxiety." This approach allows individuals to recognize the emotion's presence while maintaining a degree of detachment.

It's vital to understand that challenging emotions are not adversaries but rather messengers attempting to alert us before a significant crisis occurs. Disregarding or pushing these emotions aside may only exacerbate the challenges or lead to emotional shutdown.

Sharing personal experiences of navigating difficult emotions can be beneficial, fostering connection and letting others know they are not alone in their struggles. Moreover, seeking appropriate support and resources, such as therapy, plays a crucial role in the journey of emotional healing during tough times.

PRACTICAL TIPS FOR COPING WITH ADVERSITY

Navigating emotional healing amid adversity is undoubtedly a complex journey, demanding careful consideration and understanding of its impact on mental health. This section is dedicated to exploring practical tips for coping with adversity and steering through the intricate path of emotional healing.

Adversity is a shared human experience, touching everyone at some point in their lives. Its effects on mental health, often manifesting as anxiety and depression, are profound. Prolonged exposure to adversities can disrupt one's sense of stability, giving rise to feelings of hopelessness, helplessness, and overwhelm.

Crucially, it's essential to recognize that overcoming adversity, with the right tools and support, has the potential to fortify an individual, making them more resilient. Annie Miller, a licensed psychotherapist, emphasizes that adversity can catalyze positive changes in the brain when supported appropriately, fostering learning and personal growth.

Research highlights diverse strategies and coping mechanisms used by individuals facing adversity. Understanding these approaches equips individuals to navigate the intricate landscape of emotional healing. Practical tips encompass altering beliefs, reducing self-abuse and criticism, and cultivating persistence and endurance.

The presence of a robust support system is paramount in overcoming adversity. Whether derived from friends, family, or professionals like therapists, adequate support offers guidance, validation, and healing from traumatic events.

Moreover, recognizing and validating emotions stands as a pivotal facet of the emotional healing process. Strong emotions are a common response to difficult times, and acknowledging rather than pushing them away is crucial. Through this acknowledgment, individuals can effectively process painful life experiences, paving the way for a happier, more joyful life.

The subsequent section will delve deeper into practical coping tips for adversity, offering insights from the perspective of a therapist.

TRANSFORMING BELIEFS AND CULTIVATING SELF-COMPASSION

The journey of emotional healing post-abuse is a deeply personal expedition, unique to each individual. While the road may vary, there are strategies that can offer support and contribute to the restoration of emotional well-being.

A cornerstone of this healing process is establishing a robust support network. Surrounding yourself with understanding and compassionate individuals can be pivotal, providing not only encouragement but also validation throughout your healing journey. Seeking therapy, facilitated by an unbiased and professional therapist, offers a safe space to explore and challenge beliefs about yourself, others, and the world, differentiating between those that serve you and those that no longer do.

Understanding the dynamics of emotional abuse is a crucial step toward healing. It's possible that behaviors once deemed normal were, in fact, abusive. Deepening your comprehension of emotional abuse empowers you to recognize and process what you've endured, fostering clarity on what a healthy relationship should entail and enabling you to build stronger connections in the future.

Remind yourself that the emotional abuse you endured is not your fault. Abusers often manipulate victims into believing they deserve mistreatment, but this is a falsehood. You bear no responsibility for the actions of your abuser. Rebuilding self-esteem is paramount; constantly reaffirm the truth to yourself and focus on nurturing your self-worth.

Maintaining a journal proves to be a valuable tool for documenting feelings and experiences throughout the healing process. This practice aids in tracking progress, identifying patterns, and restoring trust in oneself. It's common to grapple with self-doubt after emotional abuse, and a journal serves as a testament to your journey and the strides you've made.

In addition to self-reflection, prioritize your needs and desires. In toxic relationships, you may have neglected your well-being. Now is the time to redirect your focus inward, identifying your desires and taking steps to fulfill them. This approach facilitates the rebuilding of self-esteem and the regaining of control over your life.

As you progress on your healing journey, establish boundaries and nurture healthy relationships. Surround yourself with those who respect and support you. Learn to recognize and address red flags in new relationships, prioritizing your emotional well-being.

Remember that the path to emotional healing demands time and patience. Be kind to yourself as you navigate challenges and emotions stemming from abuse. With the right support and resources, healing is possible, leading to a life filled with happiness and joy. Embrace your emotions; they are valid, and you deserve both healing and happiness.

TRANSFORMATIVE STEPS AFTER LIFE'S PAINFUL EVENTS

The idea of "processing" trauma has gained prominence recently, highlighting the importance of working through and healing from distressing life experiences. Not every stressful event qualifies as traumatic, and not everyone experiencing trauma will face enduring effects. Yet, if you've acknowledged the need to confront your past and its impact on your present, options are available.

Recognize that processing trauma isn't possible while it's happening. Under intense stress, your focus shifts to immediate survival, hindering a comprehensive understanding of the traumatic event. This survival mode is a natural response that protects you in the moment.

Once the traumatic event concludes, the process of healing can commence. Seeking assistance from trauma-focused therapists is beneficial, given their expertise and tools toguide you through this journey. Engaging in self-care practices like therapy, joining support groups, and journaling can also aid in processing trauma, allowing exploration, understanding, and the development of coping strategies.

Processing trauma is a personal journey, and everyone's path to healing is unique. What works for one may not work for another. Honor your emotions and experiences, seeking proper support and resources for your distinctive healing journey.

By addressing and processing painful life experiences, you can reshape beliefs, diminish self-abuse, and cultivate emotional healing. This journey leads to a life filled with happiness and joy, emphasizing the importance of acknowledging and honoring your emotions rather than pushing them away. Trust in your inner strength to navigate difficult times and become a beacon of light for yourself.

STRENGTHENING RESILIENCE AND FORTITUDE

In our earlier discussion, we underscored the significance of preserving emotional well-being in the facc of adversity. Now, let's explore more deeply how individuals can cultivate resilience and endurance to navigate through challenging circumstances.

In times of difficulty, it becomes imperative to devise strategies for nurturing emotional well-being. Engaging in self-care, seeking support from others, and fostering a positive mindset are effective means of building resilience. Taking a holistic approach to self-preservation—encompassing physical, mental, and emotional aspects—empowers individuals to cope with challenges and rebound with greater strength.

The role of mindset and perspective cannot be overstated in the journey toward resilience. Altering beliefs, reducing self-criticism, and embracing the process of emotional healing are pivotal steps in fostering a more optimistic outlook on life.

The rewards of cultivating emotional resilience extend far beyond mere survival. Improved mental health and overall well-being become tangible outcomes. Prioritizing emotional well-being not only equips individuals to surmount challenges but also enables thriving in various life domains, including relationships and careers.

Nevertheless, the path to building resilience is not without its obstacles. Individuals may grapple with self-doubt, fear, or a lack of support. Recognizing and addressing these challenges is indispensable to the successful cultivation of emotional resilience.

To support individuals on this journey, here are practical tips and techniques for building emotional resilience and fortitude:

VALIDATE AND HONOR YOUR EMOTIONS

Acknowledge and accept your feelings, even the uncomfortable or painful ones. Avoiding or suppressing emotions may impede the healing process.

SEEK PROPER SUPPORT AND RESOURCES

Establish a robust support system, whether composed of friends, family, or a therapist. Having someone to lean on can significantly enhance your ability to bounce back from adversity.

PRACTICE SELF-CARE

Dedicate time each day to activities that bring joy and relaxation. Whether through exercise, meditation, or pursuing a hobby, self-care is vital for maintaining emotional well-being.

CHALLENGE NEGATIVE THOUGHTS

Be mindful of negative self-talk and work on reframing thoughts in a more positive and empowering light. Shifting perspective contributes to the development of resilience and endurance.

EMBRACE GROWTH AND LEARNING

Perceive challenging experiences as opportunities for personal growth and learning. Reflect on the lessons gained and how these trials have contributed to your inner strength.

By prioritizing emotional well-being and cultivating resilience, individuals not only weather difficult times but also forge a path toward a happy, joyful life. Acknowledge that the journey toward emotional healing may pose challenges, but armed with the right mindset, support, and techniques, emerging stronger and more resilient is indeed possible.

SEEKING PROFESSIONAL GUIDANCE FOR SHADOW WORK

Facing life's challenges can make it seem like the short time that we have in a therapy session isn't enough to dig into the root of our problems. Sometimes, we end up talking about recent events like a tough talk with our boss or a stressful subway ride on the way to therapy. While these topics are important to discuss, many people seek therapy for deeper, long-standing struggles that cause significant pain and affect their overall well-being.

It's common for people to find it difficult to bring up these deeper issues. Avoiding pain is a natural human instinct, and some individuals hope that just attending therapy sessions each week will magically fix their problems. However, therapy's effectiveness depends on both the person's willingness to face their deepest struggles and the therapist's skill in guiding the process.

Acknowledging these deep struggles is tough because we often don't even realize when we're avoiding painful thoughts or experiences. We've become experts at deflecting and redirecting to survive in society. But if we keep these barriers up, the healing process won't reach us. Therapy is a collaboration between the patient's openness and the therapist's expertise.

Everyone comes to therapy with different concerns and needs, so there's no one-size-fits-all approach. However, there are key factors that can help you delve deeper into your therapy sessions, allowing you to address the core issues that led you to therapy and make real progress:

SEEK A THERAPIST WHO PROVIDES A SECURE AND SUPPORTIVE SPACE FOR YOUR SHADOW WORK

Finding the right therapist for shadow work can be challenging but is crucial for a meaningful journey. The stronger the connection and sense of safety with your therapist, the more beneficial your exploration of the shadow self can become. If you sense that the therapeutic relationship doesn't quite align, that's perfectly fine. Invest the time to discover a therapist who truly listens and validates your experiences as you explore the depths of your shadow.

FOCUS ON YOUR KEY CONCERNS DURING SHADOW WORK

Utilize therapy as a tool to explore the core of your deepest worries and challenges. If you find yourself overwhelmed with numerous concerns, consider prioritizing. Identify the one issue that has been particularly elusive or challenging for you to understand or process independently.

The therapy space is designed to cater to your unique needs. There's no right or wrong when it comes to choosing between discussing recent issues or those embedded more deeply in your personal narrative. It can be beneficial to self-reflect and ask, "which issues are currently impacting me the most?" Alternatively, if you notice that recent sessions have centered around less significant matters, it might be time to set aside your weekly concerns and address that more substantial issue awaiting resolution.

GAUGE YOUR READINESS TO WORK WITH YOUR SHADOW—ARE YOU PREPARED TO BE VULNERABLE?

In therapy, you hold the authority to bring forth what you're comfortable discussing. If you're uncertain about delving into your profound concerns, consider easing into the process.

One approach is to introduce a theme related to your concerns, such as family dynamics, intimacy, overwhelming emotions, or any unresolved struggles. Testing the waters involves bringing the thematic essence of your concerns into the therapy space, allowing you to share your feelings on the matter with your therapist. This gradual approach serves as a way to assess your readiness before fully immersing yourself in the exploration of your shadow self.

OPEN UP WHEN YOU'RE READY!

Once you've reached a point where you feel prepared to address your concern, take the initiative at a pace that suits you.

A helpful tip: don't hesitate to communicate your feelings as you share your thoughts and concerns. It's entirely normal to experience mixed emotions when discussing painful, unresolved struggles.

Expressing your emotions in the moment can turn the act of sharing into an integral part of the conversation. Allow your therapist to support you through this process.

If you have both recent and deep-seated issues to discuss, consider mentioning this at the start of your session. This way, you and your therapist can collaboratively set a loose agenda to ensure there's ample time to explore each concern in the current session and future ones.

EMBRACE THE JOURNEY, NOT JUST THE SOLUTION

Unraveling and processing pain and struggles is a gradual process. Engaging in conversation might sometimes bring relief, while at other times, it can evoke challenging emotions.

Approaching your therapy as a continuous process can provide reassurance that progress is happening, and your time in therapy is valuable. Time is a crucial element in the transformative recipe for gaining meaningful insights and making positive changes.

Granting yourself the space to heal demands courage and strength. For those who have delved deeper in therapy, have you felt closer to achieving your goals? How has this influenced your well-being, relationships, and overall perspective?

CHAPTER 8:
OVERCOMING
COMMON OBSTACLES
IN SHADOW WORK

> ## The brave man is not he who does not feel afraid, but he who conquers that fear.
>
> ### – Nelson Mandela

From my own experience, I've learned that engaging in shadow work is crucial for personal growth, although it can feel overwhelming if you're new to the process.

When you start this practice, you may encounter common obstacles such as fear of the unknown, resistance to change, self-doubt, and a lack of motivation. In this section, let's navigate through these challenges together and explore ways to make the most of your shadow work experience. I'll share tips on how to embrace your fears and overcome the barriers that have been holding you back from achieving success in all aspects of life.

CONFRONTING FEAR AND REGAINING CONTROL

The fear of the unknown is something that many of us grapple with, stemming from the anticipation of future events, anxiety about a perceived lack of control, or discomfort with unfamiliar situations. This fear can manifest in different ways, such as avoidance, physical tension, and emotional unease.

Facing the unknown is a common challenge in the realm of shadow work. Delving into our inner thoughts and beliefs can be daunting, pushing us beyond our comfort zones into the unknown.

To overcome this fear, it's crucial to recognize that we hold the reins in our journey of self-discovery. Approach each session with an open mind and a positive outlook, allowing yourself to learn more about both yourself and the world.

Moreover, be kind to yourself throughout this process. Acknowledge any fear or discomfort without judgment, reassuring yourself that you are safe. There's no right or wrong way to navigate this journey; go at your own pace.

With patience and persistence, you'll break through this obstacle and continue your path of self-discovery with newfound confidence.

One common hurdle in the world of shadow work is grappling with resistance to change. We all find solace in our familiar routines and habits, making it challenging to break away and welcome new experiences. To tackle this obstacle, consider taking gradual steps. Begin by pinpointing what you're resisting and why, then introduce small changes that gently push you beyond your comfort zone.

I've been actively working on stepping outside my comfort zone for years now. It's been a journey filled with challenges and moments of trepidation, yet the rewards have been immeasurable. Through this process, I've unearthed facets of myself and experienced growth I never thought possible.

Initially, breaking away from my comfort zone seemed daunting. I was accustomed to sticking to the familiar and avoiding anything that felt remotely uncomfortable. But with time, I realized that this reluctance was holding me back from countless enriching experiences.

I started with modest steps, such as venturing to new places or striking up conversations with acquaintances. Each small leap built my confidence, empowering me to take on more significant risks.

As the years passed, I confronted larger challenges, such as embracing new roles at work or exploring unfamiliar hobbies. While nerve-wracking, these experiences brought immense joy and a deep sense of accomplishment.

Certainly, there are moments when stepping beyond my comfort zone remains a struggle. It's an ongoing process that demands mindfulness and courage to push through fears. Yet, I'm grateful for the progress I've achieved and the person I've become through it. Venturing beyond my comfort zone has led me to discover new passions, connect with incredible individuals, and live a more fulfilling life.

On your shadow work journey, remind yourself of the benefits these changes bring—increased self-awareness and personal growth. Additionally, practice self-acceptance and acknowledge your current situation. Be open to moving away from it when necessary. With a positive mindset and an open heart, you can overcome this obstacle and continue on the path of self-discovery and transformation.

DEALING WITH DOUBTS: BEING KIND TO YOURSELF

Sometimes, in shadow work, we face self-doubt—those thoughts that say we're not good enough. But here's the thing: you don't have to let those thoughts control you.

First off, acknowledge those doubts without being too hard on yourself. Remember that just because you think something, it doesn't make it true. You have the power to choose what to believe about yourself.

Next, give yourself a little love. Think about what makes you awesome—your strengths, the things you've achieved, and what makes you, well, you. Mistakes? They're just chances to learn, not reasons to feel down. And if you ever need a hand, don't be shy to ask for help.

Stick with it, be strong, and you'll break through those self-doubt barriers. Your journey to discovering your best self is worth it!

DISCOVERING YOURSELF AND STAYING MOTIVATED: SIMPLE TIPS FOR SUCCESS

Staying motivated during shadow work can be a bit tough, but there are simple tricks to keep you going. First off, set small goals and break down the big ones into little steps. Celebrate the small wins and don't forget to take breaks when you need them.

Talk to yourself in a positive way. Remind yourself why you're doing this work and why it really matters to you. And hey, if you ever feel stuck, it's totally okay to ask for help. Whether it's talking to a therapist, coach, or joining a support group, getting guidance can make a big difference.

EXPLORATION OF THE UNCONSCIOUS AND THE TRANSFORMATIVE POWER OF REFLECTIVE SELF-EXAMINATION

Initially, the concept of "shadow work" may be perceived as a pursuit associated with edginess, self-centeredness, and potentially harmful magical practices. Contrary to this impression, it constitutes a significant facet of contemporary psychology and plays a pivotal role in attaining mental well-being and emotional balance.

While it may seem commonplace, the impact of shadow work extends significantly within spiritual and magical circles. The entirety of our minds and hearts, including the most concealed shadows within us, shapes our interactions with ourselves, others, communities, traditions, deities, and magical practices. These elements, in turn, exert influence on our minds and hearts, reaching into the depths of our most-deepest shadows.

Without a thorough understanding of the elements residing in your shadow, a complete comprehension of yourself, as well as the reasons behind your beliefs and actions, remains elusive.

Shadow work involves confronting the gritty, painful, and challenging aspects of your psyche associated with trauma, pain, avoidance, fear, anger, shame, hubris, and other "negative" emotions. This process revolves around bringing to light those concealed or buried parts of yourself, whether intentionally or unintentionally, to foster conscious awareness. Through this awareness, these facets can be addressed, healed, or otherwise dealt with.

Committing to shadow work is simultaneously daunting and immensely rewarding. It serves as a transformative journey wherein you gain a profound understanding of yourself, aligning your complete being with your truest self. This path leads to inner peace, self-respect, self-love, and self-realization. It offers a route to overcome or effectively manage aspects of yourself that evoke frustration, pain, and shame.

SHADOW WORK CAN BE INTIMIDATING

Tackling your shadow, those hidden and tough parts of yourself, can feel really scary. They ended up in the shadows because, at some point, you might have wanted to ignore them, couldn't deal with them back then, or they just seemed too big to handle all at once.

In your shadow, you've got the roots of coping habits that once helped in tough times but now might be causing problems. It's also where learned behaviors, like biases or ways of interacting, hang out.

Your fears, doubts, and that inner voice that brings you down live in the shadow too. It's the place of reactions that puzzle you, and even the awesome parts of yourself you've learned to hide.

Facing all this isn't a walk in the park, but just think about how amazing it could be if you did. Picture a version of yourself free from destructive habits, anxiety-causing skeletons, and fully embracing who you truly are.

Sure, it's not a quick or easy journey, but it's doable, and trust me, totally worth it.

WHAT'S CRITICAL INTROSPECTION?

Critical introspection is like taking a close, honest look at yourself without getting caught up in emotions or judgments, like saying something is good, bad, or feeling angry or ashamed. It's about consciously digging into why you think, act, react, believe, and have certain opinions.

With critical introspection, you're basically going to the roots of all those thoughts and behaviors. Once you figure out what's at the core, you can make some real changes. You get to adjust your thoughts, behaviors, reactions, beliefs, and opinions to better match who you really are and who you want to be.

Think of it as checking out your inner self, all the way to the core, and doing it with a sharp, analytical eye. It's called "critical" because you're really getting into the nitty-gritty of what, why, when, and how you are.

TAKE IT ONE STEP AT A TIME WITH SHADOW WORK

Shadow work can be a lot to handle. If you attempt to tackle multiple issues or, even worse, everything all at once, you're likely to feel overwhelmed and may find yourself sinking in a sea of seemingly insurmountable problems.

Think of it like being on a boat in an ocean filled with garbage when you start shadow work. To make progress, you need to pull some of that garbage out of the water and either reclaim, reform, recycle, or dispose of it. It's easiest to manage if you bring up a small amount of garbage at a time, so you can fully understand it and deal with it effectively.

Trying to work on your entire shadow in one go is like pulling up so much garbage that you can't move around the ship, reach the controls, or adjust the sails. The weight of the garbage threatens to sink the ship. Yes, you've brought it all to light, but what's the point if you can't effectively examine or deal with it because you're too busy just trying to survive under its weight?

Dealing with one set of issues tends to lead to uncovering another set naturally. Emotions, traumas, and responses are often interconnected and complex. Deal with the first thing you bring up. When you're ready, then tackle the next set, and so on. This approach makes it more manageable. Plus, when life gets busy, and you don't have the emotional energy for shadow work, it's relatively easy to set aside for later.

If you're using magic to enhance your shadow work, be specific about what you're addressing or how much you want to address at a time. Simply include the intent of "no more than I can handle right now." Magic follows intent, and when applied to your own psyche, it's surprisingly easy to impatiently want to fix everything at once. Take care not to overwhelm yourself. Shadow work is tough, and it takes time, so give it the time it needs.

EMBRACE YOUR SHADOW: IT'S NOT A BAD THING

The aim of shadow work should never be to completely erase your shadow. It's a crucial part of your psyche, helping you compartmentalize and navigate pressing matters despite trauma, pain, and hardships. It plays a key role in coping with the inevitable challenges and stressors that come with being alive. The trouble arises when you let things linger in the shadows, allowing them to fester and negatively impact other areas of your life.

Shadow work isn't a one-time task; it's a lifelong journey. You're continually adding to your shadow, and there's always something from the past waiting to be uncovered. Despite your best efforts with boundaries, shielding, and warding, life's challenges can find their way into your shadow. Moreover, traumas and coping mechanisms often have multiple layers, so you might discover new aspects years after you thought you had dealt with something. Ongoing shadow work is what keeps your shadow ocean clean and healthy, even as it continues to harbor undiscovered aspects.

JUDGMENT-FREE CRITICAL INTROSPECTION IS CRUCIAL

When you begin to get into shadow work or engage in critical introspection, the natural inclination is to critically judge everything. It's understandable, as the things in your shadow are likely sources of guilt, shame, fear, or anger. You might already perceive them as "bad," reinforcing the tendency to judge them negatively.

While this judgment may seem logical, it's counterproductive. Rather than healing your issues, being judgmental reinforces their root causes, making them more deeply ingrained. Piling negative judgment onto something you already feel guilty about intensifies the guilt and hinders addressing the core issues causing it.

The elements residing in your shadow must be examined and addressed as they are. Approaches such as toxic positivity, spiritual bypassing, and judgmental behavior won't make these aspects miraculously disappear.

Saying, "It is bad that I feel guilty for being awkward in public," solely focuses on the negativity of guilt and overlooks its cause. "I am awkward in public, which makes me feel guilty," reframes the issue, allowing for targeted solutions. Emotions aren't chosen; we simply feel them. "Awkward in public" becomes a challenge that can be addressed over time and with effort, whether through accepting your awkwardness, working to be less awkward, or a combination of both.

If struggling with self-judgment, consider making it the first aspect of shadow work to address. Steering clear of self-destructive judgment and showing compassion to yourself is crucial for successful critical introspection and shadow work. This approach is likely to have positive impacts on various aspects of your life.

GROWING THE SKILL OF CRITICAL INTROSPECTION

In the beginning, critical introspection might feel like a skill you're not good at—I certainly felt that way. Despite the frustration with slow progress, looking back, I realize it was a blessing. The gradual development keeps the work from becoming overwhelming and prevents the temptation to tackle too much at once.

As you continue, you'll become more adept at critical introspection. You'll learn how much you can handle at a time. You'll refine the art of asking yourself the right questions and understanding the answers. Over time, you'll become more skilled at addressing root problems and making the necessary changes to find peace within yourself.

It never becomes effortless, but you do improve, and that improvement makes a tangible difference in your life.

These questions are just suggestions based on what I ask myself during critical introspection. Your questions may differ, and that's perfectly okay. Your life and your psyche are unique. The crucial part is to pose questions to yourself and provide lovingly honest answers, even if it's a simple "I don't know."

Additionally, there's no strict order for these questions. I've roughly arranged them in the sequence I often use, but in reality, I don't follow every question or this order every time. Unfortunately, there's no one-size-fits-all method or roadmap for effectively addressing every shadow aspect. Adaptation is key for each issue. Remember to steer clear of judgmental evaluations and maintain compassion for yourself.

IDENTIFYING THE VISIBLE PROBLEM: SPECIFICITY IS KEY

The visible problem is essentially anything about yourself causing pain, difficulty, or concern. Examples include being "awkward in public," knee-jerk responses to situations, intense emotional reactions to minor events, bad habits, self-destructive thoughts or behaviors, self-deprecating thoughts or behaviors, denial of self (related to gender, sexuality, neural type, mental health, etc.), cultural conditioning (such as manners, racism, morals, religion), and more.

To make this more effective, be specific about what you want to address. If self-destructive behaviors are a concern, focusing on the entire category might be overwhelming. Instead, choose a more precise and manageable focus like "Stop pushing away friends" rather than the broader "self-destructive behavior." You can even narrow it down further by selecting a single behavior that tends to alienate friends.

For those working on not judging themselves, the visible problem and focus might be something like "I judge myself and my emotions as 'good' or 'bad' too frequently" or "I need to extend to myself the same compassion I give to other people." Specificity helps in creating a more targeted and manageable approach to critical introspection.

UNDERSTANDING THE SIGNIFICANCE OF THE PROBLEM

Evaluate how this problem brings you pain or difficulty. Be honest and explore as many "why" answers as possible. Recognize that more aspects may surface as you dive into the problem.

For the "awkward in public" issue, it might cause embarrassment, difficulties in talking to strangers, a feeling of being scrutinized, a sense of being ignored, uncertainty about the authenticity of friendships, freezing up under attention, and so on.

This question is like drilling down, uncovering a complex network of issues and garbage. Remember that it's not necessary to process everything immediately. The key is to acknowledge all those "whys" to gain insight into what may need to change for healing. You might even discover a different problem that requires attention first, and that's okay. Don't forget about the rest, but pick one to focus on.

Being excessively judgmental, for instance, leads to dwelling on negativity, hinders progress by fixating on moral judgment instead of problem-solving, fuels self-criticism instead of constructive change, exacerbates depression and anxiety, erodes self-worth and confidence, fosters self-destructive behaviors, and can lead to accepting abusive behavior as deserved. Understanding these aspects helps in developing a strategy to address and overcome the problem.

ACKNOWLEDGING YOUR FEELINGS ABOUT THE PROBLEM

Being nonjudgmental involves recognizing and respecting your feelings about the problem, whatever they may be. Take a sincere approach to acknowledging your emotions. The results of doing so may surprise you and contribute significantly to your understanding and growth.

EXPLORING THE CAUSES OF THE PROBLEM: UNCOVERING ROOTS

Now, let's dive deeper into the shadow and search for the roots of the problem. It's possible that one specific event triggered the problem, there might be a series of events, or you may have no clear idea about its origin. There's no wrong answer here, and if the problem is significant, it may take time, possibly years, to unravel it all.

Understanding the cause is crucial because it paves the way for healing. Consider if your problem arises from a coping mechanism that once helped you survive a traumatic situation. If you solely focus on the mechanism, it's akin to treating an infected wound without cleaning it or applying antibiotics. It might scab over and even scar, but it will continue to itch and reopen because the underlying infection has been allowed to fester.

By examining and healing the root issues, you increase the likelihood of genuine recovery and a lasting transformation of the problem. Addressing the roots also often leads to the resolution of other visible problems connected to the same origin.

EVALUATING THE SIGNIFICANCE OF THE PROBLEM: IS IT REALLY A PROBLEM?

When you examine the "why" and "what," you might discover that the issue isn't as severe as you initially thought. Consider whether you perceived it as a problem due to external influences, societal norms, or conditioning, especially if you belong to marginalized communities or pursue unconventional spiritual paths.

Take a moment to reflect on whether the problem is genuinely a concern for you or if it's more about meeting others' expectations. If it's the latter, scrutinize those expectations and conditioning; you might uncover the actual problem that needs your attention. While it's essential to be considerate of others in society, remember that, ultimately, you are accountable to yourself.

Upon examining the "what," "why," and "how" of your problem, you might realize that it actually makes sense and serves a purpose in your current situation, even if it has some drawbacks. Behaviors often come with both pros and cons that can be weighed and mitigated as needed.

If you find that the problem is reasonable or even beneficial in certain ways, accept and make peace with it. Focus on minimizing its drawbacks rather than viewing it solely as a problem that needs fixing.

IMPLEMENTING CHANGE TO ADDRESS THE PROBLEM: REAL-WORLD WORK

This is where the rubber meets the road, and real-world work comes into play. It often involves the challenging task of changing patterns and habits. The changes you seek may require engaging in uncomfortable or even frightening activities. Take it slow, and don't give up on yourself, even when faced with setbacks or significant obstacles. If you genuinely desire to fix the problem, you must commit to the work, recognizing that this journey is seldom a straightforward or smoothly paved road.

In the wise words of Yoda, "Do, or do not." However, he may have forgotten to mention that the process of doing so can be lengthy, filled with temporary setbacks. Nevertheless, as long as you are still in the process of doing it, you are on the right path.

ASSESSING THE WORTH OF CHANGE: IS IT A GENUINE DESIRE?

Consider whether every aspect of the problem genuinely needs to change. The process of change might demand that you sacrifice something valuable, or it may be an aspect you genuinely don't want to alter. Evaluate the pros and cons of making the change, and consciously understand why you might be resistant to it. This way, any reluctance can be addressed, preventing it from becoming an excuse to push the problem back into your shadow self, where it can be ignored while festering. Understanding the worth of the change ensures that your efforts align with your sincere desires.

DETERMINING THE RIGHT TIMING: CAN I TACKLE THIS RIGHT NOW?

After examining your problem and identifying the necessary changes, it's crucial to assess whether, at this moment, you have the emotional, mental, and physical energy to implement those changes. While procrastination should be avoided, consider the overall context of your life. Intensely focusing on shadow work shouldn't come at the cost of other essential aspects of your life.

If the timing isn't ideal, decide whether to proceed with smaller steps or pieces of the problem or if it's more fitting to concentrate on an easier, entirely different issue. There's no shame in setting something aside to address later, as long as it doesn't become an excuse to indefinitely avoid dealing with it. Be compassionate with yourself and recognize that pacing and timing play vital roles in effective personal development.

ACHIEVING PEACE: WHAT NEEDS ACCEPTANCE AND HOW TO ATTAIN IT

This question can be among the most challenging to answer, as making peace with something you deeply wish to change is no easy task. However, it's crucial to accept the aspects of yourself that are inherent and cannot be changed.

Furthermore, the answer to this question is dynamic and may evolve over time. You might make peace with a past trauma, experience closure, and not think about it for a while. However, encountering a trigger or reminder could bring up a new aspect or the entire trauma, requiring renewed attention, like a scar that pulls and needs care once again.
There are instances where you make peace with something because you're not yet in a position to undertake the work needed for healing. Later, when you are ready, that peace can be lifted so you can engage in the necessary work.

Sometimes, making peace is the genuine path to healing, moving forward, or feeling whole. It's a process that requires acknowledgment, compassion, and an understanding that acceptance doesn't mean resignation but can be a powerful step toward genuine transformation.

SEEKING PROFESSIONAL HELP

If you have the ability and desire to seek professional help, consider interviewing prospective therapists and psychologists either before or during the first appointment. Not all professionals are equally skilled, and finding the right fit is crucial for effective therapy. Create a checklist of things that matter to you or concerns you may have about potential judgment. Go into the process with a clear idea of the answers you want or don't want.

During the interview or initial sessions, consider asking about their approach to therapy, experience with issues similar to yours, their views on specific treatment modalities, and their overall philosophy. Assess their communication style, empathy, and how comfortable you feel sharing with them.

If, after this process, you find that the professional is not the right fit for you, don't hesitate to try someone else. Building a strong and trusting therapeutic relationship is essential for the effectiveness of therapy.

I know firsthand that getting into shadow work can be a real challenge. If you ever find yourself struggling with overwhelming emotions or confronting past traumas that seem too much to handle on your own, I want you to know that reaching out for help is not only okay but a powerful and courageous move.

I encourage you to consider seeking support from professionals who specialize in shadow work. Therapists and counselors trained in these areas can offer invaluable guidance and a caring presence on your journey. Remember that asking for help is a testament to your strength and commitment to self-care, not a sign of weakness.

As psychologist Guy Winch wisely puts it, just like we go to the doctor for a physical checkup, our minds deserve the same care. You've got this, and there's strength in acknowledging when you need a helping hand.

CHAPTER 9:
BUILDING AND MAINTAINING MOTIVATION IN SHADOW WORK

In this chapter, I aim to offer you a collection of motivational tips, strategies, and real-life examples that have personally resonated with me on my journey of self-discovery through shadow work. The path of introspection and self-awareness can be challenging, often demanding a steadfast commitment to face the hidden aspects of ourselves. I understand the difficulties that may arise and want to share insights that have fueled my own determination during tough moments.

One strategy that has consistently propelled me forward is setting small, achievable goals. Rather than overwhelming ourselves with the enormity of shadow work, breaking it down into manageable steps makes the process more digestible. Celebrating each small victory, no matter how minor, reinforces the commitment to the journey and builds momentum.

Moreover, I'll explore the significance of self-compassion in this process. Acknowledging that setbacks are inevitable and that the journey is uniquely yours fosters a sense of kindness toward oneself. I'll share practical techniques to cultivate self-compassion, emphasizing its role in sustaining commitment during challenging moments.

By the end of this chapter, my goal is for you to feel not only motivated but also equipped with practical tools to persist on your shadow work journey. Remember that the path to self-discovery is a personal odyssey, and each step forward, no matter how small, is a triumph worth celebrating.

When you're going through tough times and doing that deep inner work, remember that nothing stays the same forever—good or bad. It's like the yin and yang, the ups and downs. So, even when it feels like things can't get worse, hang in there.

Tomorrow might be better, and if not, the day after could be. Just don't give up. Things won't change if you throw in the towel when it gets tough. Keep moving forward, but it's totally fine to take a breather. Taking care of yourself is crucial during this time. If you're tired, rest. If you need a break, go for a walk, watch a movie, or do something you enjoy. Be kind to yourself, but stay determined.

If it ever feels like it's too much to handle, don't hesitate to reach out for professional help. I've been there and sought help when I needed it. It doesn't mean you're not strong; in fact, it shows your strength.

Some people might think asking for help is a weakness, but it's not. If you open up, support will be there for you. We're social creatures, and having someone to talk to can make a huge difference. If there's someone in your life you can trust and who'll listen without judgment, lean on them. You're not alone in this.

THE ROLE OF MOTIVATION IN SHADOW WORK

Motivation is basically the reason why we do things—the driving force behind our actions. It's what gets you going, whether it's shedding those extra pounds or aiming for a promotion at work. In a nutshell, motivation is what propels you to take steps toward your goals. It's a complex process that involves biological, emotional, social, and cognitive forces that activate human behavior.

Moreover, motivation includes the factors that not only kick-start but also guide and sustain behaviors aimed at achieving specific goals. However, these motives are often not directly visible, so we often have to deduce why people do what they do by observing their actions.

The importance of motivation lies in its role as a guiding force for all human behavior. Knowing how motivation functions and what factors can influence it is crucial for various reasons.

Understanding motivation can:

BOOST EFFICIENCY
Knowing what motivates you can make you more efficient as you strive to achieve your goals.

SPUR ACTION
Motivation is the driving force that pushes you to take action, turning intentions into tangible steps.

PROMOTE HEALTH
It encourages engagement in health-oriented behaviors, contributing to overall well-being.

PREVENT UNHEALTHY HABITS
By understanding your motivations, you can steer clear of unhealthy or maladaptive behaviors such as risk-taking and addiction.

EMPOWER CONTROL

Motivation helps you feel more in control of your life, influencing positive decision-making.

ENHANCE WELL-BEING

Ultimately, a good understanding of motivation can improve your overall well-being and happiness by aligning your actions with your aspirations.

If you have a goal, such as losing weight or running a marathon, just wanting it isn't enough. You also need to keep going, even when things get tough. There are three important parts to staying motivated: deciding to start (activation), keeping at it despite obstacles (persistence), and putting in the right amount of effort (intensity). For instance, enrolling in psychology courses is an example of activation. Going to class when you are tired shows persistence, and how much you put into studying determines the intensity. The more you have of these, the better your chances of reaching your goal.

Motivation is our personal cheerleader, encouraging us to deal with tough feelings and old hurts, nudging us to keep going. But, let's face it, sticking to that motivated mindset can get tough, especially when things are moving at a snail's pace or when it feels like an emotional rollercoaster.

There are two main types of motivation:

INTRINSIC MOTIVATION

This is when you do something because you enjoy it and it fulfills your personal needs. Hobbies and leisure activities are examples of intrinsic motivation. It's about doing things for your own satisfaction.

EXTRINSIC MOTIVATION

This is when external factors, such as salary or praise, drive you to do something. Jobs often involve extrinsic motivation, but if you find aspects of your job enjoyable, there's also intrinsic motivation at play.

In many work situations, both types of motivation come into play. Even if you like your job, there are likely tasks you don't enjoy. This is where self-motivation becomes crucial. To motivate yourself, understand your needs and what you find rewarding. By changing your perspective, you can find motivation, both from within (intrinsic) and external factors (extrinsic), to tackle less enjoyable tasks. Instead of relying on outside sources, you make the task more rewarding for yourself.

STRATEGIES FOR BUILDING MOTIVATION

MARK YOUR GOAL ON YOUR CALENDAR

Boost your inner drive by giving yourself a deadline—a specific date to work toward. No matter what you're trying to achieve, put it on your calendar. Some goals, like delving into shadow work or exploring aspects of your inner self, may not have built-in end dates. If your goal lacks a set timeline, create one by choosing a realistic date for its completion.

For example, if you're doing your shadow work to understand and integrate your unconscious aspects, set a date by which you aim to have completed a certain phase or reflection. Create a timeline for your self-discovery journey and mark milestones on your calendar. Setting a target date not only keeps you motivated but also allows you to monitor your progress. You'll always have a clear idea of how much more you need to explore, which can greatly impact your personal growth.

MAKE REACHING YOUR GOAL A REGULAR THING

When you turn working toward your goal into a habit—a thing you do automatically—you won't have to depend so much on feeling motivated. How do you make a behavior a habit?

First, find a trigger.

Pick something you already do every day, like brushing your teeth or eating lunch, to be the trigger for the action you want to turn into a habit. Write down an "if-then" plan (also called an implementation intention).

For instance, if you want to make a habit of exploring your shadow self every day, your if-then plan might be: If I sit down with my evening tea, then I will spend 5 minutes reflecting on my thoughts and emotions.

To establish a routine for exercise, it might look like this: If I finish my morning routine, then I will immediately change into my workout clothes.

Creating this plan and putting it in writing could increase the chances of sticking to it. Start with something small!

Notice that the examples above don't say you'll analyze six chapters of deep material, watch hours of introspective videos, or spend an exhaustive hour on inner exploration.

Getting started is often the toughest part on days when motivation is low, and it's much easier when the task is small: Five minutes of reflection or putting on your workout clothes.

It's awesome to be excited and sure about reaching your goal, but sometimes being too positive might not be realistic. Not every day will go exactly as you planned, and that's totally fine. Life happens.

One way to stay motivated on tough days is to plan for them. As you think about your goal, make a list of things that could get in your way. If you're exploring your shadow self, this could include:

-Feeling overwhelmed with emotions
-Getting distracted during your self-reflection
-Facing unexpected events or stressors
-Having difficulty understanding certain aspects of yourself

Once you have your list, figure out how to handle each obstacle. How can you prepare for overwhelming emotions? Maybe you could designate a quiet space for reflection, or have a friend you can talk to when things get tough.

Now, when these obstacles pop up, instead of losing motivation, you have a plan to keep going. Keep in mind that it's okay to miss your goal sometimes, especially when facing certain obstacles.

The next time you're setting a goal for yourself, try the WOOP technique by Dr. Gabriele Oettingen. WOOP stands for Wish, Outcome, Obstacle, and Plan. What's your wish? What would happen if your wish came true? What's the main obstacle in your way? What can you do to overcome that obstacle?

ACHIEVE LITTLE WINS TO GET THINGS GOING

Naval Admiral William H. McRaven shared this wisdom during a graduation speech at the University of Texas at Austin in 2014: "If you want to change the world, start by making your bed. If you make your bed every morning, you will have accomplished the first task of the day. It will give you a small sense of pride, and it will encourage you to do another task, and another, and another." The former Navy SEAL knew what he was talking about.

Studies show that accomplishing small victories regularly can create a feeling of progress, which can lead to long-term success, especially at the beginning. No matter what your significant goal is, start by breaking it into smaller parts. If your focus is on shadow work, consider smaller goals like spending a few minutes in self-reflection each day, journaling your thoughts, or discussing your discoveries with a trusted friend.

Fun fact: Setting goals at the beginning of a new week, month, or year can naturally boost motivation. We tend to connect these time points with fresh starts, distancing ourselves mentally from any past setbacks.

KEEP AN EYE ON YOUR PROGRESS

Watching yourself make progress can really boost your motivation. There are lots of tools available to help you keep track of your goals. It could be as simple as using a to-do list or calendar where you can check off tasks or days as you finish them. Or you can try a free tool such as Trello, which lets you create a customized digital task board to break down your big goal into smaller daily, weekly, monthly, or even yearly tasks.

Another idea is to make a progress bar on a piece of poster board or paper. Put it up where you'll see it often, and fill it in as you get closer to your goal.

Try this technique: A SMART goal!

Sometimes, the most effective goals are SMART goals—specific, measurable, achievable, relevant, and time-bound. And remember, if you're focusing on shadow work, your progress might involve things such as consistently reflecting on your thoughts, exploring your emotions, or sharing your insights with someone you trust.

TREAT YOURSELF FOR BOTH THE LITTLE VICTORIES AND THE BIG ONES

Getting rewarded for our efforts feels great. But did you know that rewards can also make you more motivated and improve how well you do? Celebrating small achievements and finishing major goals can make the work you're doing more interesting and enjoyable.

You don't need big or expensive rewards. Here are some quick ideas for treats you can give yourself:

-Take a short break
-Go for a walk outside
-Enjoy your favorite snack
-Read a chapter of your favorite book
-Spend a few minutes meditating
-Listen to an episode of your favorite podcast
-Plan a night out with friends
-Play an online game
-Visit a free museum or attraction
-Have a long bath or shower
-Call a friend or family member

Take a few minutes to create your own list of rewards, so you're all set to celebrate your victories, whether they're big or small, especially if you're working on your shadow self.

BE THANKFUL, INCLUDING FOR YOURSELF

You might think that being thankful could make you just settle for things as they are. But some studies show the opposite. Feeling grateful can:

-*Encourage you to make yourself better*
-*Help you feel connected to others, like you are part of a team*
-*Keep you motivated for a long time, not just during the gratitude practice*
-*Make you want to give back to others*
-*Improve your physical and mental health, and even your sleep*

There are different ways to build a thankful mindset. Spend the first 5 minutes after you wake up thinking about all the things that you are thankful for. Even better, jot them down in a gratitude journal. Is there someone in your life who you're especially thankful for? Write them a letter expressing your gratitude, especially if you're working on your shadow self.

GET MOTIVATED BY POSITIVE PEER SUPPORT

While you're the one doing the work to reach your goals, having others around can be a big motivator.

Studies show that feeling like you are part of a team can boost your determination, involvement, and performance, even if you're working by yourself. Depending on your goal, this could mean joining a group focused on exploring your shadow self, a meditation circle, a writing group, or any community that aligns with your personal growth journey.

Also, telling someone you trust about your goal can make you more committed to achieving it. For shadow work goals, think about sharing with a friend, family member, or mentor whose opinion you value. It could be someone you trust and feel comfortable discussing your inner thoughts and emotions with.

LIFT YOUR SPIRITS

Being in a good mood is linked to doing better work and getting more done. It's not about being positive all the time, which isn't always possible. But when you're feeling a bit slow about working on your shadow self, a small mood boost can be enough to get you going.

Want some ideas for lifting your mood? You could try:

-*Spending time in nature (or at least catch some sunlight)*
-*Looking at cute pictures or videos of animals*
-*Watching funny videos on YouTube*
-*Doing some exercise*
-*Taking on a different persona (like the Batman effect)*

Remember that it's okay not to feel upbeat all the time, but a little mood lift can help you kickstart your journey into shadow work.

SHAKE UP YOUR SURROUNDINGS

Switching up where you work or reflect can give you a new perspective and a burst of motivation. It's called the novelty effect—a temporary boost that comes from changing your environment.

If you typically explore your shadow self at home, consider doing it in a cozy corner of a coffee shop. Always journaling in your bedroom? Take your notebook to a nearby park for a change. Adjust your usual route for self-reflection, or try a different method of exploring your inner thoughts and emotions.

HOLD ONTO YOUR "WHY"

Why does this goal matter to you? And why is that reason meaningful? Keep asking until you reach your ultimate "why"—the core value that's pushing your goal.

To strengthen your connection to your "why," set a daily alarm to spend a minute or two picturing what success in your shadow work would be like. Imagine how it would feel to make progress in understanding and embracing your inner self.

ADDITIONAL TIPS

- Consider joining a local Meetup group dedicated to shadow work. Meeting in person can create a sense of community and accountability.

- Explore Facebook Groups focused on shadow work; for instance, "Shadow Work Explorers" is a community where members share insights and support each other.

- Connecting with others who are on a similar journey fosters a sense of familiarity, making the process more enjoyable and sustainable.

- Sharing your experiences, breakthroughs, and challenges within the group not only provides support but also offers diverse perspectives on various aspects of shadow work.

- Engage with a licensed therapist specializing in shadow work. They can help you navigate deep-seated issues and offer professional insights.

- Hire a coach with expertise in shadow work for personalized guidance and a structured approach to your self-discovery journey.

- Professionals bring a wealth of knowledge and experience, enhancing the effectiveness of your shadow work. Their objective viewpoint can illuminate blind spots and facilitate a deeper understanding of your emotions and behaviors.

- Explore books like *The Dark Side of the Light Chasers* by Debbie Ford or *Owning Your Own Shadow* by Robert A. Johnson for in-depth insights into shadow work.

- Listen to podcast episodes from platforms such as "Sounds True," where experts share practical tips and personal stories related to shadow work.

- Enroll in online courses like "The Shadow Course" by Caroline Myss to receive structured guidance and exercises. Diversifying your motivational resources keeps your approach dynamic and prevents monotony.

- Incorporating various mediums such as books, podcasts, and courses ensures a well-rounded understanding of shadow work concepts. These resources can serve as constant reminders of the importance of your journey and provide ongoing encouragement.

Incorporating these additional tips should offer a more comprehensive guide to seeking external support for motivation in your shadow work journey.

CHAPTER 10:
INTEGRATING SHADOW WORK
INTO YOUR EVERYDAY LIFE

> *As you learn to be true to yourself,*
> *you will find that you attract people, work,*
> *and other circumstances that reflect your evolution*
> *and development*
> *— Shakti Gawain*

In this chapter, I'll be guiding you on how to practically integrate shadow work into your daily life. It's all about helping you maintain balance and continue your personal growth. Remember that shadow work isn't a one-time thing; it's an ongoing journey that can be woven into your regular routines, relationships, and activities.

Taking a moment to think about ourselves is pretty crucial, whether it's about work stuff or our personal lives. Whether you're trying something new, chasing a different job, or just thinking about setting some fresh goals, self-reflection is a cool way to get things rolling.

In the context of shadow work, self-reflection involves looking into past events with an open mind to understand and enhance your actions. This might include revisiting goals and achievements, analyzing the journey and results. It could also entail reflecting on a specific situation—how you and others dealt with it—and considering your attitude and emotions at that time.

During the process of shadow work through self-reflection, it's crucial to carefully examine both the positive aspects and the challenges. Regardless of the memories you're reflecting on, acknowledging both the ups and downs is beneficial for your mental well-being, self-esteem, and confidence. This dual perspective allows you to adapt, learn from experiences, and move forward in your shadow work journey.

CREATING A DAILY ROUTINE FOR SHADOW WORK

When it comes to shadow work, there's no one-size-fits-all approach to self-reflection—everyone is unique. The method that you choose for your practice can vary based on factors such as the time you allocate and the environment you're in. The key is to find an approach that resonates with you and suits your individual preferences and circumstances.

SHAPE YOUR SHADOW WORK WITH PROBING QUESTIONS

Define the pivotal questions that steer your self-reflection concerning habits, accomplishments, and emotions throughout the period you're exploring in your shadow work.

For instance:

- *What actions did I take to navigate through that challenging phase?*
- *How does my emotional landscape contribute to my shadow work today?*
- *Considering my experiences within this timeframe, what aspects of myself could benefit from exploration and growth in my shadow work journey?*

CHRONICLE YOUR SHADOW WORK REFLECTIONS

Document each question and its corresponding answers in a dedicated shadow work journal. The act of putting pen to paper not only releases your thoughts but also brings clarity and often unveils deeper insights. Your journal serves as a tangible record to revisit your journey as you progress through your shadow work.

If you're up for an alternative reflection method, consider audio journaling. Record yourself articulating your stream of thoughts, whether through the voice recorder on your phone or another recording device. Posing crucial questions to yourself and hearing your responses can aid in recognizing diverse thoughts and feelings. This practice allows you to find clarity, express yourself, and take note of the strides you've made in your shadow work journey.

EXPLORE BREATHING EXERCISES IN YOUR SHADOW WORK

Centering your mind through breath connection before self-reflection can enhance clarity, openness, and honesty in your shadow work. Breathing exercises serve as a valuable method to ease into the process, slow down, clear the mind, and sharpen your focus.

MEDITATE DAILY

Meditation takes various forms, so discover the ones that resonate with you in your shadow work. Consider options like reading, taking a refreshing walk outdoors, or engaging in low-impact exercises such as yoga. Each of these activities can serve as a starting point for your self-reflection practice in shadow work.

Here are a few examples of meditation techniques that you might find beneficial:

MINDFULNESS MEDITATION
Focus on the present moment, observing thoughts without judgment.

GUIDED MEDITATION
Follow a narrative or prompts to lead your mind through a reflective journey.

TRANSCENDENTAL MEDITATION
Repeat a specific mantra to achieve a state of relaxed awareness.

MOVEMENT MEDITATION (YOGA)
Combine physical movement with meditation, promoting mindfulness through poses and breath.

Exploring these methods can enhance your shadow work practice, providing diverse avenues for self-reflection.

Incorporating shadow work into your daily routine is a powerful way to maintain consistency and foster personal progress. This introspective practice can be seamlessly integrated into your life, with just 15 minutes of dedicated reflection each day.

Building a habit around your shadow work is crucial for long-term success. According to a study by researchers at University College London, habits are typically formed in an average of 66 days. Therefore, committing to doing your shadow work at the same time each day can help solidify this practice into your routine.

Mindfulness is another integral component of personal development, promoting self-awareness and presence in daily life. Begin your day with a short 5-minute mindfulness session using apps like "Calm" or "Headspace," which provide guided exercises to ease you into the practice. Extend mindfulness beyond dedicated sessions by being fully present during routine activities such as eating, walking, or doing chores.

NAVIGATING RELATIONSHIPS WITH SHADOW WORK

Discovering your shadow self in a relationship holds significant importance for a couple of key reasons.

THE SHADOW CAN OPERATE WITHOUT OUR AWARENESS

There are times when our conscious self goes into autopilot, allowing the unconscious to take the reins. This often leads to:

- *Acting in ways we wouldn't consciously choose and later regretting it.*
- *Uttering words that are out of character for us.*

- *Displaying facial expressions that convey emotions we aren't consciously experiencing.*
- *Transmitting negative energy to those close to us on a psychic level.*

OUR PARTNERS MIRROR OUR SHADOW

When we talk about the attraction of opposites, it might not necessarily refer to our partners but rather to our shadow—the contrasting and conflicting aspect within ourselves.

In every personality, there are two sides to the coin:

- *Compassionate individuals may have indifference in their shadow.*
- *Generous people may harbor meanness.*
- *Caring individuals can also be cruel.*
- *Arrogant individuals may possess humility in their shadow.*
- *Resilient individuals may have fragility.*
- *Empathic individuals might find selfishness and apathy in their shadow.*

In a relationship, it might seem natural to think that qualities like indifference and meanness would push intimacy away. However, when we fail to befriend our shadow, we risk creating distance in our intimate connection with our partner. This could manifest as eye-rolling, dependency, sarcasm, and resentment.

Constantly grappling with our internal struggles, conflicts, friction, and ongoing clashes become external realities as we continue projecting onto our relationships.

CONFRONTING OUR SHADOW SELVES WITHIN A RELATIONSHIP IS ESSENTIAL FOR RECONNECTING WITH ALL FACETS OF OUR AUTHENTIC SELVES

When we feel unseen by our partner, it's possible that the issue lies within ourselves—maybe we haven't truly seen who we are.

By learning how to embrace both the positive and negative aspects of our shadow, we not only reclaim lost parts of ourselves but also transform inner adversaries into partners.

The shadow, often viewed as a challenge, is, in fact, a gift. Engaging in shadow work becomes a means of accepting this valuable gift.

The key is to integrate the shadow, allowing yourself to become a complete reflection of who you are. In doing so, you'll experience the relief of not constantly needing to be perceived as "good," finding a newfound balance and perspective. It's not about eliminating the shadow; rather, you can discover positive aspects within the negative.

For example:

- *Indifference, when understood, may translate into compassionately safeguarding our energetic boundaries.*

- *Embracing our meanness could lead to judiciously retaining resources, such as finances, for our own self-care.*
- *Confronting fears of appearing cruel may empower us to leave relationships that we've clung to for too long.*
- *Accepting our humility might involve allowing ourselves to receive help when it's offered.*
- *Acknowledging a sense of fragility means allowing ourselves to pause and rest instead of perpetually pushing forward.*
- *Overcoming the fear of selfishness may enable us to establish healthy boundaries and prioritize our own needs.*

Imagine what your relationship could look like in such a scenario—a dynamic where authenticity, balance, and self-awareness flourish.

SHARING YOUR SHADOW WITH YOUR PARTNER CAN BE A TRANSFORMATIVE STEP IN DEEPENING YOUR CONNECTION

In a relationship, integrating the shadow provides an opportunity not just to present your authentic self but also to reclaim projections from your partner, allowing you to truly see them for who they are.

However, the crucial first step is acknowledging and being aware of your dance with your shadow. Without this awareness, it's challenging to retrieve the projections.

This isn't a free pass to dismiss the impact of your actions with a simple "that was my shadow" or a license for your partner to criticize and shame you. On the contrary, it's a call to embrace relentless self-honesty, self-responsibility, and self-compassion.

By welcoming your shadow, you reverse self-rejection and establish a connection with all facets of your being. Observing every aspect of yourself at play, without shame, reconnects you with your true self and unveils your profound brilliance.

If there are moments where an apology is warranted, offer a sincere one. Then, shift your focus to releasing the positive attributes rather than attempting to eliminate what is. This process fosters growth, understanding, and a richer, more authentic connection in your relationship.

SHADOW WORK, TAKING BACK THE PROJECTION, AND TRANSFERENCE!

Discovering yourself and improving your relationship involves a few important things:

-Try being mindful—it's like really tuning in to what's happening. This helps you understand yourself better, moment by moment.

-Writing in a journal is a great way to express yourself. Let your thoughts flow without holding back, and you might be surprised at what you find out about yourself. Think about your partner's actions that bother you and describe them using three adjectives. Figure out why these things bother you and how you're different.
-Pay attention to your feelings because they're like a window to your deeper self. By understanding your emotions, you can unlock hidden parts of yourself and improve your relationship.

MAKE YOUR RELATIONSHIPS BLOSSOM

Ever notice how you react strongly in certain situations? Maybe criticism makes you feel like your self-esteem just took a nosedive. These are your emotional triggers, often connected to your "shadow" aspects. It's like a hidden room in your heart that holds feelings you might not fully understand.

So, the first step is being a detective of your own emotions. When you sense a trigger, pause and ask yourself why. This helps you uncover those shadowy parts and understand them better.

Now, armed with this emotional detective kit, you can communicate like a pro. Instead of getting defensive, try expressing your feelings and why you're feeling that way. It's like opening a door to your emotional world and inviting others in. This makes conversations smoother and more heartfelt.

Think of boundaries as your emotional shields—they're crucial for self-care. Imagine clearly expressing what you need and where your limits are. Maybe you crave alone time for self-reflection. That's absolutely okay! Setting boundaries isn't selfish; it's a superpower for maintaining your emotional well-being.

Learn to say "no" without that guilt monster creeping in. Your needs matter, and communicating them is like giving a roadmap to others on how to treat you kindly.

We've all got a backpack of past relationship traumas. These experiences often hide in our shadows, affecting our choices without us even realizing. It's time to shine a light on them.

Reflect on past relationships. See any patterns? Maybe you always end up with partners who are emotionally distant. Journal prompts can be your trusty companions here. Ask questions like, "What am I trying to gain from this kind of relationship?" or "How does this pattern relate to my past?"

So, here's to your relationships blooming like a well-tended garden!

USING SHADOW WORK FOR PERSONAL DEVELOPMENT

Shadow work not only aims to foster your personal growth and development but can also bring about these extra advantages for you:

STRIVING FOR SELF-DISCOVERY

Self-realization, a concept rooted in Jungian psychology, involves reaching the optimal expression of your personality. Jung proposed that acknowledging your shadow self is a crucial stride toward attaining self-realization.

DEEPENING YOUR SELF-AWARENESS

Shadow work facilitates an increased awareness of one's projections and judgments. When the shadow remains unnoticed, its influence on your thoughts and behaviors can go unchecked.

Developing insight into your inclinations, even the less favorable ones, empowers you to identify when they're shaping your actions, providing an opportunity for intentional change.

HARNESSING PERSONAL EMPOWERMENT

Shadow work is more than just self-reflection; it's about taking charge of aspects of yourself that were once in the shadows of your awareness.

Consider a scenario where you habitually attribute project delays to your colleagues, only for shadow work to unveil your inclination to procrastinate. Acknowledging this revelation grants you the authority to address and rectify your procrastination tendencies, instilling a sense of control over your professional endeavors. In essence, shadow work becomes a catalyst for personal empowerment and proactive change.

PROMOTING WELL-ROUNDED GROWTH

Imagine being an excellent listener, a commendable trait. However, this strength might inadvertently lead to silence in situations where speaking up is crucial. Through shadow work, suppressed assertiveness can be brought to light, allowing you to feel at ease both in listening attentively and expressing your thoughts confidently. This process contributes to a more comprehensive and balanced personal growth, where every facet of your personality finds acknowledgment and integration.

CULTIVATING COMPASSION THROUGH SHADOW WORK

Unawareness of certain aspects of your shadow may contribute to irritation when encountering those qualities in others. Shadow work serves as a tool to unveil the connection between your reactions and concealed elements of your own personality.

Through self-reflection and introspection, shadow work enables the extension of compassion. Armed with newfound self-awareness, you're better equipped to replace irritation with understanding, not only toward others but also toward yourself. This transformative process can pave the way for a more compassionate and empathetic approach to interpersonal dynamics.

ALWAYS REMEMBER...

Shadow work offers profound opportunities for personal development, enabling individuals to evolve and unlock their full potential. One significant advantage lies in the identification of areas for growth, such as cultivating assertiveness, honing leadership skills, or enhancing emotional intelligence. By doing shadow work, individuals can unravel the impediments hindering their progress, such as the fear of rejection that may curb assertiveness.

Moreover, shadow work serves as a life changing tool for discovering one's passions and life purpose, often concealed by societal or familial expectations. Encouraging exploration without judgment, it empowers individuals to understand their suppressed desires, like a long-neglected interest in painting.

Practical experimentation with various activities, facilitated by platforms like "Meetup," further facilitates the exploration of personal interests and passions.

Integral to this developmental journey is the cultivation of self-love and self-compassion, accepting all facets of oneself, including the shadow. Engaging in daily affirmations, such as acknowledging one's worthiness of love and respect, forms a crucial component of this process.

Patience becomes paramount, recognizing that personal development is an ongoing journey rather than a fixed destination—a sentiment echoed by the wise words of Robert Louis Stevenson: "Don't judge each day by the harvest you reap but by the seeds that you plant."

By exploring these different aspects, shadow work isn't just a therapy thing—it's like a journey that can really change you. It helps you discover more about yourself and grow in a complete way.

CONCLUSION

Remember how we discovered this incredible strength that lies within ourselves? It's become our secret weapon on this journey of becoming the best versions of ourselves. It's all about facing those parts of us that we might've ignored before. And you know what? We found the strength to handle it. Give yourself a big, warm hug and say, "I accept and choose myself."

Are you ready to kickstart your self-discovery journey? This book on shadow work is your go-to guide. No need to wait—start implementing the tired and tested techniques I've hunted down for you today! Start uncovering the real you! Make it a part of your daily routine, and watch how it brings awesome benefits to your life. Get to know yourself better, boost your resilience, and find a deeper sense of purpose.

We all have fears and things that trip us up, but consider this book as a friend who knows what scares us and gives us a pep talk. It's like saying, "Hey, it's okay. We got this together." And I even shared some clever tricks to handle the tough stuff.

Remember that shadow work isn't a one-time thing; it's like a life-long adventure that we're experiencing together. This book doesn't just leave us hanging after we finish it. It's a forever companion that sticks around, showing us how to keep growing every day.

So, here's to us, my friend! May the upcoming years of our lives be full of even more cool discoveries, growth, and feeling proud of being exactly who we are.

KEY TAKEAWAYS

- *Shadow Work helps you understand hidden hurts, control your feelings, and heal your inner child.*
- *This book is an easy-to-follow beginner's guide that breaks down shadow work into simple steps, so everyone can give it a go.*

- Start seeing real changes pronto by using practical exercises from the book—it's like a quick transformation toolkit.
- Tackle challenges and keep your mojo going with lots of advice on staying motivated throughout your shadow work adventure.
- Remember that shadow work isn't a one-time thing; it's a continuous journey that fits right into your daily life, helping you grow all the time.

If you're hungry for more, this book is just the beginning. There's a whole world of resources and pros out there to help you dig even deeper. So, let this be your first step into the incredible adventure of self-discovery!

Check out *Romancing the Shadow* by Connie Zweig. It's like a guidebook with cool strategies for understanding and dealing with your shadow self. There are practical exercises and real-life stories that make it super interesting. Another gem is *Meeting the Shadow: The Hidden Power of the Dark Side of Human Nature* by the same author. It's like a collection of essays that give you different perspectives on the mysterious parts of yourself. So, grab these books, and let the exploration begin!

And hey, why stop there? Explore more works by experts such as Carl Jung, Robert Johnson, and Debbie Ford. Create your own reading list based on what tickles your curiosity!

Ready for some hands-on experience? Look for local workshops or hop into online ones. The Shift Network is a cool place that often hosts online workshops. It's like a virtual classroom with experienced guides, making your learning journey interactive and fun.

If you prefer learning at your own pace, check out courses on Udemy or Coursera. They're like treasure troves of knowledge, offering different levels from beginner to advanced. Plus, there's a bunch of live events and webinars for that extra boost of excitement!

Feeling a bit social? Connect with fellow shadow adventurers on platforms like r/Jung on Reddit. It's a place to share your stories, ask questions, and learn from others who are on the same journey.

And if Facebook is more your thing, join the "Shadow Work" group. It's like a cozy corner for sharing your progress and getting advice from your new virtual buddies. Don't forget to explore other online spots such as Discord, where you might find awesome communities sharing their own wisdom.

Your journey to a brighter you begins now. Acknowledge those shadows, find your light, and enjoy the ride. Let's get started on your shadow work journey today. I know you can do this!

The transformative power of exploring the depths of your own psyche is truly awe-inspiring. Believe in the magic that lies within the shadows—it's where true self-discovery happens. I truly believe you can navigate this tricky path and come out on top. You are not alone on this path; countless individuals have faced their shadows and emerged stronger, wiser, and more compassionate.

Accept the challenges that come with shadow work, for they are the stepping stones toward emotional mastery and a more fulfilling life. Remember that the journey may be arduous at times, but the rewards are immeasurable.

As you continue your shadow work journey, may you find solace in the knowledge that you possess the strength to confront your innermost fears and the resilience to transform them into sources of empowerment. Each step forward is a victory, and every insight gained brings you one step closer to deep healing and growth that await you.

Wishing you well on this journey of self-discovery and empowerment. May you find the courage to face your shadows, the wisdom to learn from them, and the grace to emerge triumphant. Cheers to the incredible journey that is your life!

JOURNAL PROMPTS FOR SHADOW WORK

I want to talk with you about this incredible thing that I discovered a while ago—shadow work journal prompts. They're an awesome tool, especially for those of us who are just starting out on this journey of self-discovery. They are like a magic mirror that helps us understand ourselves better and navigate through the ups and downs that we've faced.

Getting to know and embrace your shadow self is like giving yourself a big old hug. It's a form of self-care that goes beyond face masks and bubble baths (although those are great too!). Personally, it's been a game-changer for me, reshaping how I see things and boosting my mental well-being.

Starting out can feel a bit tricky, though. Trust me, I get it. That's why these journal prompts are your friendly guide. We're usually pretty good at spotting shadow traits in others, but when it comes to our own stuff, it takes a bit of digging.

All it takes is a blank notebook or journal, where you can jot down the prompts from this blog post and choose one to begin your exploration.

These prompts stimulate your thoughts and, especially when maintained in a shadow work journal, assist in unraveling your shadow traits, understanding their origins, and finding a path forward. It's a deliberate and constructive approach to self-discovery and personal evolution.

These prompts are crafted to tap into your feelings, memories, and experiences—often from your childhood—that still have a say in how you roll today, whether you realize it or not.

As you dip into these prompts, they gently nudge you to dig a bit deeper into those feelings or stories. This exploration helps you understand the roots of these emotions, understand how they might be showing up as not-so-great traits, and, most importantly, grasp your thoughts, actions, and boundaries as you move forward.

Some of these prompts might take you to a place that's not all rainbows and butterflies, and that's perfectly okay. After you've done your prompt pondering, I'd suggest a bit of meditation and self-care to process any emotions that bubble up and bring some Zen to your mind.

Whether you're using shadow work worksheets, a beginner's workbook, or just going with the flow, don't forget to keep yourself in check. If you catch yourself slipping into toxic behaviors, especially if they're affecting others, take a beat to call yourself out. But here's the thing—don't stop there. Dig into why you reacted the way you did. Is there something inside that's raising its hand for attention and growth?

Take a moment to jot down how you could handle similar situations in a different light down the road. For instance, if you've found yourself blowing up at someone close for a reason that only starts to make sense after you've spilled it onto the pages, think about how you can respond in a cooler, more collected manner if it happens again.

This, my friend, is where the genuine magic of personal growth happens. It's like unlocking a whole new level of understanding and kindness.

Choosing one journal prompt at a time not only simplifies the process but also reduces the sense of overwhelm, making it more manageable. Here are some of my personal favorite journal prompts that might help you:

PROMPTS FOR UNRAVELING WHATEVER YOU NEED TO KNOW ABOUT YOURSELF

1. Do you find it helpful to tackle one journal prompt at a time, making the process more straightforward and less overwhelming?

2. In terms of self-compassion, do you struggle to extend it to yourself, and if so, how does practicing self-compassion impact your emotions?

3. When was the last time you forgave yourself for a mistake, and what was the mistake? How did the forgiveness process unfold?

4. Can you list five self-care activities that provide you with a sense of safety and security?

5. Reflecting on past experiences, can you write about a time when someone showed you compassion? How did it make you feel?

6. Similarly, have you ever shown someone else compassion? If yes, why did you do it, and how did it feel?

7. During which situations are you hardest on yourself, and where do you believe this self-critical tendency originates?

8. Why do you think you might be reluctant to be kind to yourself?

9. Describe a time when you put yourself under unnecessary pressure. What do you think motivated this, and were external pressures, like parental expectations, a factor?

10. What specific situations tend to make you feel less than or not good enough? And why do you believe these feelings arise?

11. Reflect on a time when you made a mistake and needed forgiveness. How did the situation play out?

12. In terms of physical well-being, what types of body movement bring you comfort?

13. Can you identify three ways you could be kind to yourself today?

14. Regarding your relationships, how do you go about setting and enforcing boundaries? What are those boundaries?

15. Reflect on your emotional response when people overstep your boundaries.

16. What are the three main goals you want to achieve through shadow work?

17. Considering Jungian archetypes, which one do you most identify with, and what is the reason behind this identification?

18. Is there anything you are currently avoiding or in denial about?

19. How do you personally define the concept of "love"?

20. Have you ever found yourself manipulating others for self-protection? If so, when did this behavior start, and how does it make you feel?

21. What is one regret you have, and why is it a regret? How do you feel about it now, and do you think it's something you can correct in the future?

22. When you were a child, did your parents show you compassion and forgiveness?

23. Reflect on the morals and values your parents or caregivers instilled in you. How do your current morals and values align with these, and why?

24. Describe your relationship with your parents or caregivers, and how is your current relationship with your family?

25. Think back to a time in your childhood when you felt wronged. How did you react, and how has this affected you in adulthood?

26. Can you articulate your core values as a human being, and what is more important to you? What are you morally passionate about?

27. How do you perceive failure, and how does it make you feel? How did your parents react to failure?

28. What parts of your parents or caregivers do you see in yourself? When did this become apparent, and how does it make you feel?

29. Reflect on any toxic traits you've noticed in your parents. How does being aware of these traits affect you?

30. How do you feel about the statement, "Parents are human beings. They aren't perfect or super-human. They make mistakes and mess up just as much as you or I"?

31. In terms of emotional processing, how did you handle emotions as a child, teenager, and young adult?

32. How do you process emotions now, and has this approach changed over time? If so, how?

33. What preconceptions do you have about femininity, and where do you think these preconceptions originated?

34. What preconceptions do you have about masculinity, and where do you believe these preconceptions came from?

35. How were you taught to deal with emotions as a child?

36. Reflect on any unanswered questions from your childhood.

37. Is there something you've always wanted to confront someone about but haven't? Why didn't you confront them, and how do you feel about it now?

38. Describe a time when someone you trusted betrayed you. How did it make you feel at the time, and how do you feel about it now?

39. Write about a traumatic event in your life and explore how it has impacted you.

40. Consider a significant life event that you believe you've moved on from. How do you think you managed to move on?

41. If you could speak to someone who broke your trust now, what would you say to them?

42. Recall a time when someone you looked up to let you down.

43. How do you feel about who you are as a human being?

44. Define your attachment style and explore how you think this attachment style formed.

45. Do you struggle to form healthy attachments within your relationships? If so, why?

46. Would you describe yourself as self-destructive? If so, how do you engage in these behaviors?

47. When you experience emotional pain, how do you typically make it go away, and how do you feel about this coping mechanism?

48. Write about one person you've never forgiven. What did they do, why do you still hold a grudge, and do you want to forgive them someday but can't bring yourself to?

49. When you feel emotional pain due to past trauma, where in your body do you feel it stored?

50. What is one thing you can do today to release some of the trauma stored in your body?

51. Reflect on the most hurtful thing anyone has ever done to you.

52. Describe the most hurtful thing you've done to yourself.

53. How do you move forward after hurting someone else?

54. What's the biggest promise to someone else that you've broken?

55. What's the biggest promise to yourself that you've broken?

56. Have you ever had your heart broken? Write about it. How do you feel about it now?

57. Have you ever broken someone else's heart? Write about it.

58. How do you fill your time when bored?

59. How would you LIKE to fill your time when bored?

60. List at least five things that bring you enjoyment.

61. Who were your heroes growing up, and what did you admire about them?

62. What's the meaning of life to you?

63. What was the last argument you had about, how did you react, and how do you feel about it now? Was it resolved?

64. How do you feel about confrontation, and why do you think this is?

65. What was one way you used to self-soothe when you were growing up?

66. What were your hobbies when you were younger?

67. What are some ways you can bring activities you enjoyed as a child into adulthood?

68. If you could speak to your child-self now, what would you say?

69. How does thinking about yourself as a child make you feel?

70. When you feel threatened or cornered, how old do you feel, and did anything traumatic happen at this particular age?

71. Do you often experience physical reactions to emotional stress? If so, write about these.

72. If I told you to sit with your feelings instead of avoiding or numbing them, how would this make you feel?

73. Are you more prone to fighting, flying, freezing, or fawning? Why do you think this might be?

74. How do negative experiences impact your intimate relationships?

75. What are your "comfort movies" or TV shows?

76. How often do you find time to yourself? Do you wish to improve this, and if so, how can you?

77. What are your limiting beliefs, and how do you plan to overcome these?

78. What are three traits in others that you dislike?

79. Do you have a tendency to project traits you don't like onto others because you potentially possess them yourself? If so, which traits and why do you think this is?

80. What are some shadow traits that you know you possess, and how do these make you feel about yourself?

81. Why do you consider certain shadow traits you possess to be "negative"?

82. What's one trait that you see in other people that you wish you had, and why?

83. Do you often find yourself over-thinking things you've said or how you've acted? What usually triggers this?

84. What tends to trigger envy within you? Why do you think this is?

85. If your shadow was a separate person, what would you say to them?

86. How do you react when you're angry? Does this reaction reflect the way you saw others react to anger growing up?

87. What triggers you, and can you identify your main triggers?

88. Do you ever find yourself acting 'out of character'? When does this tend to occur the most?

89. What are your toxic traits, and how do they present themselves?

90. What aspects of yourself would you like to improve, why, and how do you plan to do this?

91. Has anyone else ever pointed out areas that you need to improve? What were these, and how did this make you feel?

92. What emotions do you tend to avoid feeling?

93. What negative emotions are you actually quite comfortable sitting with? Why might this be?

94. What is the biggest lie you've ever told someone else, and how did it make you feel to tell it? What were the ramifications of this lie?

95. What's one lie you tell yourself consistently, and why do you tell it?

1. Which aspects of self-care tend to be neglected by you?

2. What prompts you to overlook your self-care routine?

3. In what ways do you demonstrate self-care and concern for your well-being?

4. Which essential need do you frequently deny yourself, and how does this deprivation affect your emotions?

5. What personal anecdotes shape your perception of your own worth?

6. What messages did you receive regarding having your needs met, and do you believe they were fulfilled during your childhood? If not, what was lacking?

7. What experiences from your childhood contribute to feelings of unworthiness?

8. Were you comfortable requesting what you needed as a child, and how did your caregivers respond to such requests?

9. How do you handle the violation of your boundaries? Do you establish and communicate boundaries, or do you avoid conflict?

10. How much weight do you give to your own validation compared to the opinions of others? Would you compromise something important to you for the sake of others' approval?

11. In what areas do you exert minimal effort when it comes to yourself, and how could you approach them differently?

12. Reflect on your understanding and connection to qualities often associated with identity. How do these concepts influence your sense of self, and what emotions arise when contemplating them?

13. What challenges do you currently face in prioritizing yourself, and what strategies will you use to make a change?

14. Recall instances of invalidating words when expressing boundaries or concerns in the past. Do you still treat yourself similarly, and what advice would you give to your younger self?

15. Do you believe your needs are significant, and how do you communicate this belief?

16. Compare how your caregivers treated you to how you treat yourself now. Are there similarities, and how do you feel about them?

17. Were you raised to prioritize the needs of others, and how has this impacted you?

18. How do you manage your emotions, particularly the negative ones?

19. Reflect on your caregivers' treatment of you versus how you treat yourself now. Are there parallels, and what are your feelings about them?

20. How do you perceive your body, and what steps can you take to enhance its care?

21. Identify your triggers on bad days and create a to-do list to uplift your mood.

22. How can you effectively communicate your needs with others?

23. List kind words about yourself without guilt, and place them in visible spaces.

24. In what ways do you prefer to receive and express love, and how can your loved ones support you?

25. Describe your ideal morning routine.

26. Consider your authentic self versus your people-pleasing self. How do they differ in behavior?

27. What positively influences your mental health, and when do you notice a decline?

28. What have you been procrastinating on, and what's the underlying reason?

29. Identify your biggest fears and take a step today to confront one that challenges you.

30. Explore and confront false beliefs you hold, and find ways to challenge and change them.

31. What is the root cause of your anxieties, and how can you work toward healing?

32. Examine the source of recent negative behavior and plan steps to change it.

33. Identify the cause of your unhealthy patterns and develop strategies to break them.

34. Explore the triggers for your feelings of unworthiness and work toward overcoming them.

35. Identify unresolved issues from the past and seek ways to heal them.

36. Find the source of your inner pain and work toward releasing it.

37. Reflect on the lesson you can learn from your current struggles and how you can grow from them.

38. Identify the cause of your self-sabotaging behavior and develop strategies to overcome it.

SHADOW WORK PROMPTS FOR RELATIONSHIPS

1. What fears am I holding onto that are preventing me from connecting more deeply with my partner?

2. How do I sabotage my relationships?

3. What emotions am I avoiding in my relationships?

4. What do I need to let go of in order to be more present in my relationship?

5. What are my expectations of my partner and how do they limit us?

6. What triggers my fear of intimacy?

7. How can I accept my partner's flaws and imperfections?

8. What do I need to stop expecting from my partner?

9. How can I learn to trust and be vulnerable in my relationships?

10. What patterns from my past relationships am I bringing into this one?

11. What can I do to become more emotionally available to my partner?

12. How can I communicate my feelings without being defensive or blaming?

13. What can I do to foster a healthy give-and-take in the relationship?

14. How can I break the cycle of criticism and judgment in the relationship?

15. How can I show more appreciation and gratitude to my partner?

SHADOW WORK PROMPTS FOR SELF-LOVE

1. What do I need to do to nurture my own self-love?

2. What do I admire about myself?

3. What have I learned about myself that I didn't know before?

4. What do I need to forgive myself for?

5. What does self-love look like for me?

6. What do I need to do to start loving myself more?

7. What steps can I take to practice more self-care?

8. What are the ways that I can learn to accept myself?

9. What is holding me back from loving myself?

10. How can I show myself more compassion?

11. What would I do if I loved myself unconditionally?

12. What would I do differently if I felt more confident in myself?

13. How can I start being kinder to myself?

14. What do I need to do to start believing in myself?

15. What changes do I need to make to start respecting myself?

SHADOW WORK PROMPTS FOR TRAUMA

1. What are the ways in which I have been avoiding my trauma?

2. What are the ways in which I have been protecting myself from feeling the pain of my trauma?

3. What are the ways in which I have been avoiding addressing the issues that led to my trauma?

4. How have I been avoiding healing from my trauma?

5. What are the ways in which I have been numbing myself from my trauma?

6. What are the ways in which I have been avoiding facing my trauma?

7. What are the beliefs I have about myself due to my trauma?

8. How has my trauma affected my relationships with others?

9. How have I been using avoidance mechanisms to avoid my trauma?

10. What is the true source of my trauma?

11. What can I do to create a safe space for myself to begin healing from my trauma?

12. What kind of support do I need to start healing from my trauma?

13. What are the areas of my life that have been affected by my trauma?

14. What are the triggers for my trauma that I need to be aware of?

15. What are the positive changes I can make in my life to help me heal?

SHADOW WORK PROMPTS FOR LETTING GO

1. What in my life do I need to let go of in order to move forward?

2. What beliefs do I need to let go of that are holding me back?

3. What experiences do I need to let go of in order to heal?

4. What emotions do I need to let go of to be free?

5. What relationships do I need to let go of in order to be healthy?

6. What patterns do I need to let go of to make space for new possibilities?

7. What fears do I need to let go of to feel empowered?

8. What mental stories do I need to let go of to be present?

9. What habits do I need to let go of in order to grow?

10. What judgments do I need to let go of to be compassionate?

11. What expectations do I need to let go of to be more content?

12. What resentments do I need to let go of in order to be at peace?

13. What doubts do I need to let go of to trust myself?

14. What unhealthy attachments do I need to let go of to be independent?

15. What comparisons do I need to let go of to be happy?

As you go through these prompts, pay close attention to your responses. When undertaking new challenges, it's common to default to familiar patterns, even if they are less than ideal. Here are some tips to help you continue making progress with your shadow work:

1. *Maintain an Open Mind*
2. *Practice Self-Compassion*
3. *Exercise Patience*
4. *Dedicate Undivided Time*
5. *Reflect on Your Progress*

Approaching your shadow work with an open heart, self-compassion, and a patient mindset will enhance the depth and effectiveness of your journey.

Acknowledging both your light and dark sides is about living in the middle, not denying the shadow but getting to know, integrating, and loving it. This practice fosters healing, honoring the vulnerable, depressed, or fearful aspects of yourself. Approaching your shadow with love and acceptance not only benefits you but also enhances your tolerance for imperfect behaviors in others. It's a journey toward becoming a more rounded, compassionate human being.

AFFIRMATIONS FOR SHADOW WORK

Affirmations serve as uplifting statements and brief, motivating phrases that individuals can vocalize daily, offering valuable support during personal challenges or when seeking inspiration. Commonly known as positive self-talk, these affirmations are crafted to transform negative thoughts into more constructive ones, fostering positive transformations. Engaging in this practice can contribute to heightened confidence, enhanced self-worth, and a reduction in anxiety for many individuals.

In fact, mental health counselors often suggest incorporating positive affirmations into a patient's therapeutic routine. This approach can assist patients in gaining a more rational outlook on challenging situations and embracing their current reality as part of their healing journey.

The impact of these expressions varies, shaped by an individual's core values, personal history, goals, interests, and aspirations. Serving as poignant reminders, these affirmations are designed to reconnect the speaker with their desired identity and the aspirations they aim to achieve.

We all deserve to bask in the warmth of love, especially from within. These affirmations for self-love will not only nurture your self-esteem and value but, most importantly, shower you with the love that is rightfully yours.

Cultivating self-love is a pivotal element for a joyous life. When we harbor love for ourselves, navigating through life becomes a seamless journey. There's no room for judgment, fear, or dwindling self-esteem; instead, there's an abundance of gratitude and compassion toward our own beings.

The beauty of self-love extends beyond personal fulfillment; it nurtures healthier connections with those around us, creating a harmonious and mutually beneficial dynamic.

Self-love affirmations are a powerful tool in harnessing the magic of positive language to reshape our mindset. Consider the uplifting impact of kind words from others on your self-esteem. Now, envision being the source of that encouragement for yourself with the transformative power of self-love affirmations!

The practice of daily positive affirmations serves as a powerful tool against negative thinking, which can lead to chronic worry, anxiety, and depression. These declarations of intent or aspiration should ideally be recited daily, with each affirmation repeated 10 to 15 times. Whether using well-established affirmations or crafting personalized ones, these positive expressions reinforce self-worth and exert a positive influence on thoughts and behaviors. Ultimately, individuals should choose mantras that resonate with their identity and align with their aspirations.

DAILY AFFIRMATIONS FOR SELF-LOVE AND SERENITY

1. Today, I embrace and love myself just as I am.

2. I consciously choose kindness and gentleness toward myself.

3. I am my own greatest ally and friend.

4. Love flows naturally from me to myself.

5. I express gratitude for the unique person I am.

6. Every part of me is worthy of love.

7. I honor and appreciate my life.

8. My uniqueness is a source of strength and bcauty.

9. I acknowledge and embrace my awesomeness.

10. I genuinely love the person I am becoming.

11. In all situations, I am calm and relaxed.

12. My muscles release tension effortlessly.

13. With every deep breath, calmness washes over me.

14. I am at ease in the company of others.

15. Thankfulness and gratitude fill my heart for the goodness in my life.

16. Peace and tranquility envelop me as I breathe deeply.

17. I release all negative emotions from my being.

18. A peaceful and loving life is my rightful and deserved reality.

19. Slow, deep breaths fill me with a profound sense of calm.

20. I release worries and fears, making space for happiness and joy.

21. I am comfortable with the pace of my life.

22. Peace and pleasant emotions are my constant companions.

23. I redirect my focus to joyful experiences.

24. I acknowledge the temporary nature of my feelings and situations.

25. Serenity and tranquility are my inherent states of being.

26. My thoughts slow down, bringing clarity and peace.

27. Each breath anchors me to a relaxed state of mind and body.

28. Relaxation enhances my problem-solving abilities.

29. I reclaim my personal power in every situation.

30. I am naturally free from stress.

1. The Universe has my back, ensuring my higher good.

2. Everything is unfolding perfectly; I trust in the journey.

3. Taking life one day at a time, one step at a time.

4. Harmony and balance flow through every aspect of my life.

5. Letting go of stress is a natural and effortless process.

6. I choose to immerse myself in feelings of peace.

7. I am inherently good, deserving of happiness, health, and peace.

8. Accepting what I cannot change brings me inner peace.

9. Good things consistently manifest in my life.

10. Relaxation is my default state of being.

11. I am inherently worthy of all the good things life offers.

12. Inhaling confidence, exhaling fear—I am in control.

13. Unconditional self-acceptance is my constant practice.

14. Endless strength resides within me.

15. I am far stronger than I often realize.

16. I possess the power to confront any challenge.

17. My inner strength is boundless.

18. No matter the situation, it will be okay in the end.

19. Handling everything with ease is my natural ability.

20. Supporting my best self is a continuous learning journey.

21. Each passing moment brings a deeper sense of calm.

22. I am deserving of kindness from myself.

23. I navigate life one step at a time with confidence.

24. I am the master of my thoughts and in control.

25. I take pride in my accomplishments.

26. Capably managing my responsibilities is second nature.

27. I allow myself the time needed for healing.

28. Stress has no hold on me; I release it effortlessly.

29. Every part of my body is relaxing, and I am at peace.

30. Gratitude fills my heart for the entirety of my life.

SELF-ESTEEM AFFIRMATIONS FOR SELF-LOVE

1. My body is a comfortable and nurturing home.

2. All is well in my world; I am calm, happy, and content.

3. I listen to my body's messages with love and understanding.

4. I am deserving of all the goodness life has to offer.

5. Positive thoughts contribute to my healthy and happy body.

6. Everything is aligning for my highest good.

7. I make decisions that empower and serve me well.

8. Independence and control are my birthright.

9. I am worthy of positive and fulfilling experiences.

10. Calmness embraces me with every breath I take.

11. Unconditional self-acceptance is my daily practice.

12. I handle every situation with ease and confidence.

13. My life is a constant blessing.

14. Strength and confidence are my natural states.

15. I allow myself to authentically be who I am.

16. Lightness and ease fill my being.

17. Everything is under control; I trust in the process.

18. Positive and healing energy surrounds and uplifts me.

19. I have all that I need to navigate this day successfully.

20. Today and every day, joy is my chosen state of being.

SELF-CARE AFFIRMATIONS

1. I prioritize self-nourishment in mind, body, and soul.

2. In my own life, I am a valuable and essential priority.

3. Living in the present moment, I take each day as it comes.

4. My self-care is a daily commitment worthy of my time.

5. Treating my body as a temple, I honor it with respect.

6. I have the right to fulfill all my needs and desires.

7. Responsibility for my well-being is a task I embrace.

8. Self-care is a vital aspect of my life.

9. Daily, I focus on nurturing my body, mind, and soul.

10. Caring for myself is as important as caring for others.

1. At this moment, I am safe and secure.

2. Strength is building within me with each passing second.

3. Gradually, I open up to the calmness within.

4. The truth is, I am surrounded by blessings, love, and support.

5. My strength surpasses my own perception.

6. I trust the unfolding process of life.

7. Life consistently works in my favor.

8. My body is at ease, and tranquility prevails.

9. Every part of my body relaxes as I embrace peace.

10. Safety and control are my inherent states.

11. Gratitude fills my heart as I appreciate the goodness in my life.

12. I possess the resilience to overcome setbacks.

13. Belief in my ability to navigate tough times empowers me.

14. I am surrounded by love and support.

15. I accept myself and invite peace into my heart and mind.

16. Here and now, I believe in my capabilities.

17. Healing is a continuous process, and I am on that journey.

18. Love for myself is my guiding light.

19. I am deserving of all the good things life has to offer.

20. Self-respect and kindness are the foundations of my being.

1. I tune into the wisdom of my innermost self.

2. The truth of my childhood is revealed to me.

3. I choose to forgive those who have caused me pain.

4. Releasing the burdens of my childhood, I find freedom.

5. In this present moment, I am safe and secure.

6. Love surrounds me; I am a vessel of love.

7. I am whole, and my completeness is my strength.

8. Perfect in my imperfections, I embrace myself.

9. My inner child dances in joy and carefreeness.

10. New discoveries bring healing, and bitterness is released.

11. I navigate through tough emotions with courage and resilience.

12. Joy and the carefree spirit of my authentic self are my birthright.

13. Gratitude fills my heart for the presence of my inner child.

14. My spirit is nurtured, and my essence is cherished.

15. With love and grace, I hold my inner child close.

16. I am not defined by what happened to me.

17. Safety and security envelop me; I am shielded from harm.

18. I am enough, just as I am.

19. My voice is valuable, and I deserve to speak my truth.

20. I allow my emotions the space they need, acknowledging their validity.

21. I am attuned to the wisdom within me.

22. I sit with myself, embracing the child within, ready to heal.

23. Love flows within me, directed toward myself.

24. Strength resides in me, a wellspring of inner power.

25. Beauty radiates from the core of my being.

26. I release the need for perfection and forgive myself.

27. Forgiveness extends to those who have wronged me, setting me free.

28. Self-acceptance is my gift to myself; I embrace who I am.

29. Vulnerability is safe, and I allow myself to be open.

30. I fully experience and embrace my emotions; it is a safe journey.

31. The innocence of my inner child deserves love and compassion.

32. Trust is restored within my inner child.

33. Trust extends beyond; I am open to trusting others again.

34. Speaking my mind is my birthright; I am worthy of being heard.

35. I am deserving of care and nurturing.

36. Love and grace envelop my inner child, providing comfort.

37. Safety surrounds my inner child; they are protected.

38. Love embraces my inner child; they are cherished.

39. Wholeness defines my inner child; they are complete.

40. Perfect just as they are, my inner child radiates beauty.

41. Gratitude accompanies every step of my healing journey.

42. Willingness to heal is a powerful force within me.

43. Love and light flood my being; I am filled with warmth.

44. I celebrate my journey toward healing with joy and gratitude.

45. I am in full control of my life's direction.

BIBLIOGRAPHY

Anahana. (2023, October 8). What is Shadow Work - Start Healing Your Unconsciousness. https://www.anahana.com/en/wellbeing-blog/mental-health/what-is-shadow-work

Applegate, D. (2023, March 26). Shadow Work and Self-Discovery: Overcoming Common Obstacles - Rediscovering Sacredness. *Dominica Applegate.*

Bence, S. (2023, June 14). All about grounding: techniques to connect to nature. *Verywell Health.* https://www.verywellhealth.com/grounding-7494652

Bullet Planner Ideas. (2023, June 7). The Best Shadow Work Exercises for Healing. *Bullet Planner Ideas.* https://bulletplannerideas.com/shadow-work-exercises-for-healing/

Cherry, K. (2023, May 3). Motivation: the driving force behind our actions. *Verywell Mind.* https://www.verywellmind.com/what-is-motivation-2795378

Cleveland Clinic. (2023, August 1). Tap into your dark side with shadow work. https://health.clevelandclinic.org/shadow-work

Cooks-Campbell, A. (2002, March 15). How inner child work enables healing and playful discovery. *BetterUp.* https://www.betterup.com/blog/inner-child-work

Cotec, I. (2021, December 30). Shadow Work and Healing the Inner Child (In 5 Steps). *HeroRise.* https://www.herorise.us/shadow-work-and-the-inner-child/

Coursera. (2023, November 29). How to motivate yourself: 11 tips for self improvement. *Coursera.* https://www.coursera.org/articles/how-to-motivate-yourself

Cozolino, L. (2014). *The neuroscience of human relationships: Attachment and the developing social brain* (2nd ed.). W. W. Norton & Co.

Dbojic. (2023, November 19). 88 Affirmations for Shadow Work: A Journey to Wholeness. *Positive Affirmations.* https://positiveaffirmationscenter.com/affirmations-for-shadow-work/

Dietsch, A. M., et al. (2014). Perceptual and instrumental assessments of orofacial muscle tone in dysarthric and normal speakers. JRRD 51: 1127–1142.

Diggory, T. (2020, December 16). How to practise self-reflection. *Calmer.* https://www.thisiscalmer.com/blog/how-to-practise-self-reflection

Ebede, F. (2023, November 20). 100 Shadow Work Prompts: A Guide to Shadow Work Healing. *Sselfhealjourney.com.* https://selfhealjourney.com/2023/02/24/shadow-work-prompts/

Eileen, S. (2020, August 5). Shadow work and the magic of critical introspection. *The Balancing Path*. https://sidneyeileen.com/2020/08/05/shadow-work-and-the-magic-of-critical-introspection/

Elizabeth, D. (2023, April 24). 44 Affirmations for Your Inner Child: Nurture and Heal Childhood Traumas. *Wild Simple Joy.* https://wildsimplejoy.com/affirmations-for-your-inner-child-healing/

Gathege, M. (2023, November 7). Navigating emotional healing during difficult times: A therapist's perspective. *Medium*.

Giovanni. (2020, May 27). Meeting your shadow self through meditation. *Live and Dare*. https://liveanddare.com/your-shadow-self-and-meditation

Goldstein, E. (2023, November 11). What Is an Inner Child | And What Does It Know. *Integrative Psychotherapy Mental Health Blog*. https://integrativepsych.co/new-blog/what-is-an-inner-child

Goyal M, et al. (2014). Meditation programs for psychological stress and well-being: A systematic review and meta-analysis. *JAMA Intern Medicine* 174 (3): 357–368.

Griffiths, N. (2023, May 10). 100 Shadow Work Journal Prompts for Healing, Self-Awareness & Growth. *Seeking Serotonin*. https://seekingserotonin.com/shadow-work-journal-prompts/

Harewood, S. (2023, October 19). Shadow Work: How to strengthen your relationship with yourself and your partner. *Sandra Harewood Counselling*. https://sdhcounselling.co.uk/shadow-work-how-to-strengthen-your-relationship-with-yourself-and-your-partner/

Ho DYF. (2014). A self-study of mood disorder: Fifteen episodes of exuberance, none of depression. *Spirituality in Clinical Practice* 1 (4): 297.

Hölzel BK, et al. (2011). Mindfulness practice leads to increases in regional brain gray matter density. *Psychiatry Research 30* (191): 36–43.

Inner Journeys. (2023, July 9). Shadow work. https://innerjourneys.life/shadow-work/

Jerath R, et al. (2006). Physiology of long pranayamic breathing: Neural respiratory elements may provide a mechanism that explains how slow deep breathing shifts the autonomic nervous system. *Med Hypotheses 67* (3): 566–571.

Kabat-Zinn, J. (2003). Mindfulness-based interventions in context: Past, present, and future. *Clinical Psychology: Science and Practice 10* (2): 144–156

Keohan, E. (2022, September 14). How to Cope with Trauma. *Talkspace*. https://www.talkspace.com/blog/how-to-deal-with-trauma/

Khoury B, et al. (2013). Mindfulness-based therapy: a comprehensive meta-analysis. *Clinical Psychology Review 33* (6): 763–771.

Kurtz, A. (2021, September 2). How meditation helps you heal (Plus, a simple breathing practice). *Yoga Journal*. https://www.yogajournal.com/meditation/meditation-classes/using-meditation-heal-chronic-illness/

LaVine, R. (2023, October 20). 100+ Deep Shadow Work Prompts to Accept Yourself and Move Forward. *Science of People*.

Lee, K. A. (2023, October 11). 5 essential reasons to practice grounding before you start *Any* shadow work. *The Moon School*. https://www.themoonschool.org/shadow/5-reasons-grounding-before-shadow-work/

Lockett, E. (2023, March 27). Grounding: Exploring earthing science and the benefits behind it. *Healthline*. https://www.healthline.com/health/grounding#benefits

Mateo. (2023, September 24). Shadow Self: 13 Types & How to Embrace Your Dark Side. *LonerWolf*. https://lonerwolf.com/shadow-self/

McKnight, J. (2023, August 13). Shadow Work Meditation Script | Step by Step Guide 2023. *Planet Meditate*. https://planetmeditate.com/shadow-work-meditation-script/

McLachlan, M. (2022, September 13). What Is Breathwork? An Introduction to the Art of Breath Control. *Ancient + Brave*. https://ancientandbrave.earth/blogs/news/what-is-breathwork-an-introduction-to-the-art-of-breath-control

Mejia, Z. (2023, May 3). 10 Science-Backed Benefits of Meditation. *Forbes Health*. https://www.forbes.com/health/mind/benefits-of-meditation/

MindTools. (n.d.). https://www.mindtools.com/awk1tdw/motivating-yourself

Paler, J. (2023, September 15). Shadow Work: 7 Steps to Heal the Wounded Self. *Hack Spirit*.

Perry, C. (2015, August 12). The Jungian Shadow. *The Society of Analytical Psychology*. https://www.thesap.org.uk/articles-on-jungian-psychology-2/about-analysis-and-therapy/the-shadow/

Quinn, J. (2021, February 2). How to Do Shadow Work & Reclaim Your Authenticity. *Consciousness Liberty*.

Raypole, C. (2023, September 15). 30 Grounding techniques to quiet distressing thoughts. *Healthline*. https://www.healthline.com/health/grounding-techniques#soothing-techniques

Regina. (2022, July 22). Shadow Meditation: Befriend your darkness. *Rituals of Healing Mindful Psychotherapy*. https://ritualsofhealing.com/blog/embracing-your-dark-side

Rose, K. , & Rose, K. (2022, July 14). 25 fun & simple summer activities to heal your inner Child. *Kee Rose*. https://www.lifewithkeerose.com/heal-your-inner-child/

Shiken.ai. (2023, November 15). 8 Benefits of shadow work and how to start practicing it. https://shiken.ai/personal-development/shadow-work

Siegel, D. J. (2010). *The mindful therapist: A clinician's guide to mindsight and neural integration*. W. W. Norton & Co.

Spohn, N. (2023, September 22). 3 Empowering shadow work Exercises for beginners - From dark to light. *Let Your Shadow Shine*. https://letyourshadowshine.com/shadow-work-exercises-for-beginners/

Tang YY, et al. (2007). Short-term meditation training improves attention and self-regulation. *Proceedings of the National Academy of Sciences USA 104* (43): 17152–17156.

Telloian, C., et al. (2022, May 26). Shadow work: The self-improvement technique designed to boost awareness of yourself and others. *Insider*. https://www.insider.com/guides/health/mental-health/shadow-work

Tewari, A. (2022, December 17). 100 Self-Love Affirmations for Higher Self-Esteem. *Gratitude— - the Life Blog*. https://blog.gratefulness.me/20-affirmations-to-say-to-yourself-when-you-need-support/

Thompson, E. (2023, January 30). Recess break! 10 yoga poses your inner child will love. *YouAlignedTM*. https://youaligned.com/yoga/inner-child-poses/

Villines, Z. (2023, November 8). What is shadow work? What to know. *Medical News Today*. https://www.medicalnewstoday.com/articles/what-is-shadow-work

Weingus, L. (2022, September 12). 35 Shadow Work Prompts for Beginners. *Silk + Sonder*. https://www.silkandsonder.com/blogs/news/shadow-work-prompts-for-beginners

Zeidan F, et al. (2010). Mindfulness meditation improves cognition: evidence of brief mental training. *Conscious Cognitive 19* (2): 597–605.